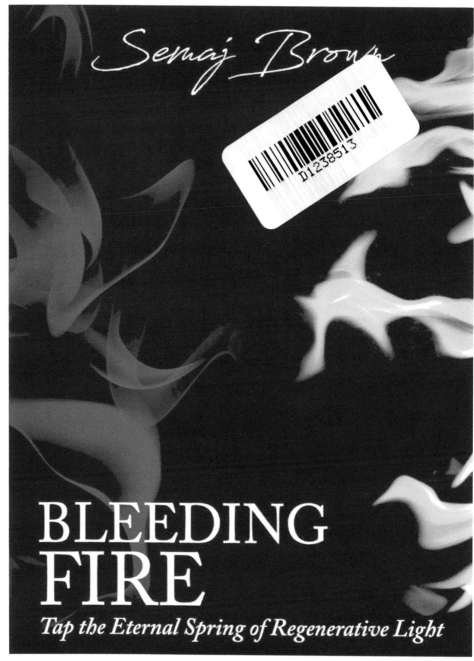

Semaj Brown

BLEEDING
FIRE
Tap the Eternal Spring of Regenerative Light

Conversations in Poetry and Prose

BLEEDING FIRE

Tap the Eternal Spring of Regenerative Light

Conversations in Poetry and Prose

Semaj Brown

Bleeding Fire! Tap the Eternal Spring of Regenerative Light

© Copyright 2019

Publishers: Broadside Lotus Press and Health Collectors™ LLC

International Standard Book Number 978-0-9857766-1-9

Library of Congress Control Number TXu 002-136-390

www. BroadsideLotusPress.org

or Health Collectors™ LLC

1109 Linden Rd. Bldg. B Ste. 2

Flint, Michigan 48532

Email: Semajrooted@gmail.com

DEDICATION

This book is dedicated to my husband, Dr. James Brown, who often asked me, "Why don't you have a book?" The first time I heard the inquiry, my mind went blank. Then, a conveyor belt of projects and responsibilities sped through my head. Images of education workshops and the twenty-one-year stretch of direct care I provided to very ill family members did a fast rewind. Our move from Michigan to Kentucky and then back reminded me of a million paper cuts, and my dance with brown boxes. Memories of developing programming for our Health Collectors LLC, supporting the medical practice, studio recordings, stage productions, playwriting, and serving the community as if the community employed me to work a 60-hour work week rushed through my brain as a blur.

My husband had very clear ideas about the book he wanted me to write: "It should contain all your writings," he said with grand gestures. "Poetry, prose, philosophical commentary, curricula you have designed, the recipes from the *Planted Kingdom* cookbook— everything!" I thought aloud, "What kind of book would that be?" He answered, "A book that has never been written!"

I knew, by the glint in his eye, that he was on a mission to convince me to write this book. He was persistent. He cajoled and encouraged and nurtured this idea, offering arguments and explanations as to why this was the thing to do, now.

My beleaguered brain began to open slowly, making a space for the idea. After many weeks, I confided to him, "I am going to write a book of poetry and prose. The title will be *Bleeding Fire! Tap the Eternal Spring of Regenerative Light.*

My husband had excavated a long ago dream from wherever forgotten dreams are stored. I am deeply grateful to him for his original insistence and the immeasurable contribution he made through all of our subsequent conversations concerning the content and concepts in this book.

ACKNOWLEDGEMENTS

I recognize and bow to vastness beyond my comprehension. I am grateful for infinity force, for wind, the breath of Earth, for ablution rain, and for the glint of sun star. I thank God, the creator, the ultimate infinity, swirling parent of ancestors and grace.

 About a decade ago, I was listening to a National Public Radio (NPR) series on the creative processes of famous writers. A common thread among the authors was admiration for their editors. They discussed the sometimes difficult but necessary process that helped to transform very good writing into great writing. Longingly, I listened. I yearned to experience the tug and subsequent polish of the editing ritual. I mused to myself, hmm, but first, I must have a book to edit!

This book has had the benefit of two editors who are also very dear friends. They are my sisters. I am forever grateful to professor emeritus of Wayne State University and University of Michigan, Senior Editor of Broadside Lotus Press, 2019 Kresge Eminent Award recipient, Gloria House (Dr. Aneb Kgositsile, PhD), and to retired Literary Arts High School educator, and fiction writer, Ms. Darolyn Brown, MA.

Darolyn, the consummate teacher, disrupted my sport of collecting semi colons, calling foul, blowing the whistle on errant grammar. Like a good referee, this former debate coach and nine-times *Excellence in Education* recipient, reviewed and posed questions that incited me to probe deeper meanings — which resulted in additional writings and revisions.

Aneb approached the work with the skill and precision of an elite neural surgeon whose tool was a tiny laser scalpel. Her intellectual incisions were delicate. Words were tweezed like the lifting of fine hair, and then ever so slightly shifted as to not disturb the voice of the original work. She cleared micro-pathways for meanings to shine unobstructed. She brought 50 years of professional literary experience to bear on my NPR longing.

I thank Dr. House and the board of Broadside Lotus Press, Chris Rutherford, president, for welcoming *Bleeding Fire! Tap the Eternal Spring of Regenerative Light* into the rich literary history of the Broadside Lotus Press legacy.

Amanda Thomason, graphic designer and fine artist, worked through many versions of the cover. Our shared process of conceptualization uncovered many layers of meanings, which she then translated into a layout with visual clarity. Thank you, Amanda.

I am forever grateful for the insistence of my brilliant, loving husband, James Brown, MD: "You must write a book of poetry and prose!" I appreciate his subsequent collaborations which are chronicled in the dedication section.

My sister, Lynn, who is a fountain of resilience, was time keeper, reminding me of what I was running out of, keeping me on course, and encouraging the process throughout. She embodies the spirit of tenacity which has been an inspiring example.

Cousin Linda and I have been connected since before we turned our names around at age of 4 or 5: The name Adnil did not stick, but obviously Semaj did. Cousin Linda is electrical grounding for my high voltage creative current. She is the safe place that reminds, "It's all in divine order." This is a shout out to the entire Richardson family and to new baby, Noah!

Thank you, Brown family, for showing support — by showing up! Your being there means everything to me and James. Geraldine, thank you for bringing the term *asset* into my personal stratosphere.

Linda Overton, my Grambling State University roommate, keeper of trust, listened to my early work, secret poems late in the night. Linda taught me about the rams in those bushes. Her faith is unwavering. She still holds to her college dream that one day we will be interviewed by Oprah.

Thanks to John Henry, President of the Flint Institute of Arts, who recognized my poem, "Mother Ocean: Making of a New Tribe," as something special, and invited me to present it at the Tenth Annual Community Gala (January 2017). This performance sparked my return to my public poetry life. Thank you, Gloria House, PhD, of Detroit Independent Freedom Schools Movement (DIFS), who recognized the writing of "Mother Ocean…" as a gift, and invited me to benefit DIFS and the Charles H. Wright Museum of African American History (CWMAAH) with my original production, "By Ocean, By Fire: An Odyssey of African American History and Culture" (2017). Thank you, Charles Ferrell, vice president for public programs at the Charles H. Wright Museum of African American History, for inviting me to debut the *Bleeding Fire* publication, and hold a book signing at the CWMAAH, May 18, 2019.

I thank my Facebook community, including my Cass Tech class and Pamela Purifoy, who is friend, and a stellar social media brander. I am thankful for the friendship of former Timbuktu Academy of Science and Technology educators. I heartedly appreciate the support of Susan A. Kornfield. I am inspired by her legacy of goodness. I thank Chene Koppitz for conversations and media eye. As president of Flint Chapter Pierians, Inc., I am grateful for the embrace of my sister Pierians. I could not have asked for a kinder group of nurturing, creative souls. I am forever grateful to my Zeta Phi Beta Sorority, Incorporated family: Outstanding leaders Elner Taylor, Leslie Wilson Smith, Angela Hardison, and Angela Philmore and all my sisters who create the brilliant royal blue fire that keeps me a blaze! I am grateful to be able to collaborate with the young artists of Al Nur African Dance Troupe and their director, Ayi Robeson. The children of Al Nur are the promise of the future.

Thanks to the women who stand, gather round, lift up, sip tea with me on occasion, tell truths to one another, and surround me with warmth and love: Pamela Purifoy, Velynda Makhene, Sunonda Samaddar, Mildred Smith, Aurora Harris, Nelda Hebert, Andrea Richards, Linda Belford, Nannette Dupree, Elner Taylor, Elicia Baker, Edith Withey, Linda Williams, Cindy Campbell, Elizabeth Jordan, Aneb Kgositsile, Diane Kirksey, Michelle Jahra McKinney, Rita Muhammad, Jasmine Murrell, Jeannette Murrell, Sharon Simeon, Arlene Williams, Linda Richardson, and Linda Overton.

CONTENTS

FOREWORD

I am continually amazed by my wife Semaj's journey as a literary artist, educator, performer, inspirational storyteller, and community builder. Her excursion into the world of words began when she was a child. Her mother, Mrs. Bessie L. James, supplied young Semaj a daily diet of legacy poets from Dudley Randall's Broadside Press. Their enjoyment of poetry was accompanied by appreciation of a wide range of literary works, treks to Stratford, Ontario to see Shakespeare's plays, violin lessons, basement science laboratory explorations, visual arts classes, museum visits, and lots of theater. This upbringing, steeped in broad cultural experiences, taught Semaj an appreciation for global civilizations through her mother's Pan-African lenses, and created the foundation that has produced her distinct 21st Century poetic voice.

Semaj's poems appeal on a multitude of magnetic levels — conscious, subconscious, and preconscious. Pulling from both left and right brain modalities, she is a science-driven artist who sees art in science, science in art, and poetry in everything — as you will discover in this collection.

Approaching Semaj's work, one mines densely layered lines to arrive at new ways of seeing and understanding experiences. Often these insights are rendered through powerful allegorical characters that appear from other worlds, and linger forever in our consciousness. This feature of her work is particularly evident in her poems, "Mother Ocean: The Making of a New Tribe" (2017), and "The Stolen Cocoa Bean Head" (1997).

In other instances, Semaj emphasizes the musicality of language. Having been a student of the violin for years, she hears tones in speech patterns that she translates into the tonal melodies of her poems. "Wave Rock," an anthem that protests oppression, illustrates this technique, with its rhythm of repeated phrases, rhyming vowels, and clashing consonants reverberating to appeal on a subconscious level. In a major departure from the free verse of most of her poetry, Semaj turned to hip hop rhythms in her poetry curriculum for women, *Butterfly Building: A Self-actualization Program for Women* (2012).

Following Semaj's performance of "Mother Ocean…" at the *Charles H. Wright Museum of African America History* in 2017, I realized her work should be recognized along with her literary peers of this generation, and to that end, Semaj needed to write a book. It was as if I was overcome by a new mission to convince my wife to create a book that would include aspects of all her varied types of writings -- poetry, allegory, fantastical tales, cultural commentary -- to document her important contributions to African American culture.

What has been consistent throughout all of Semaj's writing is the theme of fire. At the beginning of this year, she told me that the name of the book I had urged her to write would be: *Bleeding Fire! Tap the Eternal Spring of Regenerative Light*. The title struck me on a subconscious level. My reaction was visceral. Then, Semaj asked me what the title meant to me. I told her, "The blood reference signifies our racial memory, our DNA, which is encoded in all of the children of the African Holocaust.

The fire reference is the imagery of the force of imprinting, of branding that accompanies the power necessary to pass these memories on to the next generation so that we may rise, never forgetting the atrocities we have suffered as a people." In order not to forget my spontaneous response, I went to the computer and typed it immediately.

Readers of this collection become like prospectors searching for gold. The creative revelation will be so close you will feel the energy vibrating through your mind — metal detector. Semaj's writings show us how to mine the goal of justice, purify our intentions, and shine with brilliant freedom. Her work clarifies how to *Tap the Eternal Spring of Regenerative Light*. Bright light is found in the *Me Too* section of this book. In the poem, "ROAR, Rhymes of Applied Rights," she gives our little girls a new chant, a new way to play, rhyming their power into reality. In the poem, "When Fools Talk to Me," Semaj shines a nuclear light, suggesting we fight the bigotry of "micro-aggressions," as there is nothing micro about covert racial verbal assaults.

Tap into the Eternal Spring of *Regenerative Light* for me is instruction. It means that within all of us, individually, and as a collective, we have Soul Force, God Power, Blood Fire, Universal Energy, and the will to overcome our oppression by accessing our spiritual best selves.

Readers will be thrilled to hold *Bleeding Fire! Tap the Eternal Spring of Regenerative Light* in their hands, and drill into the meanings and metaphors that will lift and transport them to other realms.

James Brown, MD
February 11, 2019

PREFACE

Dear Beautiful People:

I understand you are the angel people, the beautiful people I know and those I have yet to meet, who ignite hope, and extinguish doubt. You work with grace and grit to organize, and to rebuild what is broken. For your striving, I am deeply grateful to you.

In these difficult times, there is much to do to redeem our world. The cynics say, "Problems have always been here." I answer, "So, too, have solutions."

I know when nights and days are trauma-filled, whimsy can be a friend to the ghosts who appear in my dreams. I have found the twirling twins of Art and Science to be a benefit in clarifying paths to new thought. I believe that keeping counsel with the Tribe of Nomadic Rainbows has grounded me; but my ideas have matured in one-sided dialogues. I have missed having conversations with you.

To rectify this lopsidedness, I am reaching out to you in these pages, to explore freedom strategies, to unwind, to laugh, to cry, to pour out our hearts or remain contemplative. I am inviting you to tap the eternal spring of regenerative light.

Peace and blessings,
Semaj

"Know thy self."

Kemetic Proverb

Black Holes and the Beacon

About Black Holes and the Beacon

At 3 a.m. when computers yield deference to the moon, and screen lights dim, the arrogance of knowing fades and questions emerge. What if an individual's core or an individual's success is not as much about what acted on that individual, but more about what did not act on that individual? The writings in this section honor the primary actors of influence in my life. I refer to the institutions that helped to form me as Black holes. I call my mother the *Ultraviolet Beacon.*

I am aware, however, that there were countless other institutions, schools, family members, friends, structures, and forces that did not act on me directly, and by not acting on me directly, they became a point of great influence over my social and evolutionary development.

I heard an associate celebrate. She was ecstatic that her children are all college-educated adults. They made it. "Hallelujah! I'm through!" she exclaimed, with hands tossed high. I, too, was happy for her; but I thought of Keisha, a nine-year-old African American girl, born into the throws of abject generational poverty.

The rodents that infest Keisha's apartment are not Keisha's fault. The bowl of empty for dinner is not Keisha's fault. The shattered windows from socially engineered bullets are not her fault. Nine- year-old Keisha did not design institutional

1

racism, a system that requires an inferior educational system to ensure substandard life for the majority — to guarantee illiteracy, forcing Keisha into vulnerability, into domestic violence, into incarceration and sex traffic victimization. Nor did Keisha make the water she drinks poison. Keisha did not cut her water off for non-payment. Keisha did not make herself at risk for Hepatitis C. Yes, I thought of Keisha. I thought of our invisible caste system that ensures the expansion of poverty.

If we do not disrupt the ravages of lack, if we do not insert ourselves via talent, resources or advocacy, then we ensure, by our absence that the primary actors on Keisha's wellbeing will remain those entrenched barriers to a self-actualized life.

This is a call to those comfortable beautiful people who sleep stroll through oblivion, to those who abdicate social responsibility, not because they are inherently callous, but because their blinders are emotional protectors, or perhaps they have not allowed themselves to think deeply enough or feel far enough. Of course, there will always be those who feign ignorance: "I did not know it was this bad."

I implore the yawning beautiful people to cease visiting your den of denial. Research bares out that you will feel more enlivened and fulfilled and your life will be enriched beyond measure when you decide to become an engaged volunteer or a primary actor for positive radical change. Keisha needs you; the world needs you, and I thank you.

Black Holes: The Institutions that Shaped Me

There are beacons and there are Black holes. Beacons push out; Black holes pull in. These mysterious Black holes with vast vortexes of suctioning energy are mostly described as majestic outer space cavities, but there are terrestrial-bound Black holes too, often disguised as organizations and unlikely institutions. Black hole gravitational force is an intense consumption of all light, absorption of all color. Objects in its magnetic field disappear into a midnight sea of ink; they are drawn into the infinity of coal carbon pigment of steaming asphalt, the cooled igneous lava rock bleeding black fire.

The dominion of the Black hole is unparalleled, as Black holes have been confiscating energies from galaxies, molecular cities, and atomic villages prior to formation of epoch time. In their Venus Fly Trap world, absorption is queen, the process of transformation, the spiritual techniques involved in tapping the eternal spring of regenerative light— transmuting solid to liquid, physical to chemical, then to spiritual energy, and then retrograding infused ions into the palpable dreams of living flesh in clay bodies is coded ancestral alchemy.

My initiation into my first Black hole was during childhood. As the solo member of my spy club, I was a novice explorer, trying to break the code to something, diving for the unknown, scouring my mother's library.

I found myself teetering just outside the realm of interest, sounding out the syllables in the Gwendolyn Brooks's poem, "We Cool." I was balancing with my book on the rim of curiosity, wanting to take a peek into the flaming bowels of this nebulous, cavernous stirring, when I was shoved off the cliff of uncertainty into the blackest of holes by a sonic beacon of ultraviolet light.

The sonic beacon of light that pushed me was my mother, the legendary Bessie L. James, who you will meet in the writing, *Ultraviolet Beacon*. Mother did not believe in dawdling. She would chide, "You cannot wave to these Black hole institutions from a distance. This is not a hokey pokey ritual, sticking right toes in, and pulling left toes out. Black holes, our institutions, demand commitment as dark waves heat/fix the tortured souls of Black folk with restoration of stolen truths." She communicated with the stern conviction of an African maestro charged to conduct my life into a freedom brave and marvelous.

Free falling from the thrust, submerged in the murky soup of magnetism, spiraling into the vat of multi- dimensional darkness, I tumbled through superficial layers of my psyche, through the splattering of tone and meaning, intellectual ideas pushing upwards through my nostrils, revolutionary alphabets spilling sideways from my ears, my brain bubbling in the abyss of Dudley Randall's Broadside Press, the oldest, (since 1965), continuous publisher of African American poetry in the United States.

I nearly suffocated, but cosmic planetary pressure forced growth of gills and I swam in the poetry of legacy poets: Gwendolyn Brooks, Sonia Sanchez, Etheridge Knight, Audrey Lorde, Haki R. Madhubuti and others. During my teenage years, my poetry influencers were Stevie Wonder and George Clinton Parliament Funkadelics; in my twenties, my work was informed by Ntozake Shange and Jayne Cortez. By my thirties, I was steeped in Kahlil Gibran and Rumi; by the forties, my voice was my voice, though swept by Pablo Neruda, Garcia Lorca, Keorapetse Kgositsile, and Elizabeth Bishop.

Poured into this 1960s cooking cauldron of cultural contradictions, I dissolved into the soup of Black hole Pan African Congress, a stew of lit gases whirling primeval ancestral principles, electromagnetic justice, poetic verse, music, Vaughn's Bookstore, basement science laboratory, and lessons at Arts and Crafts before it became Center for Creative Studies. The melting of my mind was a peaceful submission. Nothing escaped, including Black hole Highland Park Chamber Orchestra, directed by my violin teacher, Mr. Joseph Striplin, who was a dedicated, brilliantly gifted young conductor, and who holds the distinction of being the first African American member of the Detroit Symphony Orchestra. There were annual summer treks to Black hole Stratford, Ontario, with Grandma Louise and Cousin Linda to study Shakespeare.

Black holes consumed me, and became me, and I achieved —
a strange equilibrium of being — the freedom to perpetually
float in fire. I remain simmering in the lagoon of literature,
music and science like a mythical creature that emerges once
every 14 years. My heart is filled with ebullient gratitude to all
of my Black hole institutions and experiences that cultivated,
molded, sculpted, and are yet forming and refining my
perspectives. I thank you Broadside Lotus Press, Vernon
Chapel A.M.E, Unitarian Universalist Church, Unity Temple,
Temple No. 1, Central United Methodist (Saturday's at
Central Art Worship Services, Rev. Ed Rowe), Girl Scout
Camp Metamora, Detroit Symphony Orchestra, Stratford
Ontario Shakespeare, Cass Technical High School's
Symphony, Harp and Vocal, Highland Park Chamber
Orchestra, Pan African Congress, Detroit Institute of Arts,
Public Radio, Horizons in Poetry, Charles H. Wright Museum
of African American History, Detroit Public Schools,
Grambling State University, Wayne State University, Shrine
of the Black Madonna Bookstore, Timbuktu Academy of
Science and Technology, The Pierians, Incorporated, and Zeta
Phi Beta Sorority, Incorporated Zeta Beta Zeta.

Story of the Ultraviolet Beacon
Gratitude to Legendary Mother, Mrs. Bessie L. James (1918-2011)

Three consecutive years of *Raspberry Interrogations* provided me with a life lesson to pass into perpetuity. "Come here, come out here I want to show you something about these raspberries." I moved hesitantly, lifting one leg then plotting down the other. Mother was out the door and in the patch in the backyard by the time I approached the porch. I wasn't really resistant; my mind moved in slow automation, one laborious step after the other. I was in a state of intense ponder. There was something about these raspberries that I should know, but could not determine specifically. This was the second year of berry questions, visiting the bushes with my mother's firm instruction.

"Now, which is the raspberry stem and which is the sucker? Look closely. Which one of these is the sucker?" My memory was tripped by her intensity. Here I was again, trying to decipher between two gangly stems that looked identical. I stared into the swaying green mother's hand had just brushed. "Look, can't you see the difference?"

Mom sounded more sympathetic. Maybe she thought I needed an appointment with Dr. Butler, our family ophthalmologist. "Which is the stem and which is the sucker? Why do they call the sucker the sucker? Do you remember?" She was leaning toward me peering up from under her bifocals.

I rolled the question around and around in my head until it became a ball, a tight knot of nothing. "I don't know," I replied shifting from one leg to the other. "Stand up, stand straight, it's good to be tall. You're not built down to the ground like me. Lift your head, focus, look closely and determine the difference." But how could I lift my head and look down at the raspberries at the same time? Though that smart-alecky thought was steeped in logic, it was only for my internal amusement. By now the sun was bright, but not hot. There was a glare and I was squinting. "Where are your glasses? Go get your glasses so you can see! Let's move it."

I skipped up the back porch steps into the house, took a flight to my room, gleeful to escape the raspberry inquisition, snatched my spectacles from the top of my dresser, and returned to the outdoor classroom. Mother had been pulling weeds. There was a pile of surrendered foliage just to the side of the raspberries. "Now, which is the sucker and which is the raspberry stem?" I selected, pinching a stem between my index and thumb, a stem that to me looked identical to the others. "This is a sucker." "No." It was finite. I am sure the answer was followed by explanation.

Years prior, while driving down the street with mom at the wheel, we had stopped at a red light. Mother instructed me to look over and down to my right. Propped up against the wall of the food market were three homeless men, who might have been mistaken for a heap of grey sacks, or bags of trash. I would never have seen them there, still as old debris, their heads appeared disembodied, melting into the slate-colored snow of March. "Do you see those men?" "Yes," I replied. I was six years old and wondering about the how and why of this ghastly sadness. I knew something was very wrong. I felt a foreboding in my soul. Mother said, "Those men are fallen stars, fallen stars." Her voice was soft, yet shrill: "Never laugh at them. They are fallen stars. Something got into them that made them that way; it could be alcohol or drugs or the war, we don't know, sometimes the mind goes bad. We pray for them and do what we can to help. Do you understand?" "Yes Ma'am," I whispered through the contracting hole in my throat. "We are no better than they are. You must pay attention to your surroundings, be aware of where you are; this is your life." The light turned green.

Mom was acutely aware, her social sensibilities were heightened, and she made me antenna-like as well. Together we deconstructed all the television programs of the era: *Tarzan*, *Little Rascals*, *Shirley Temple*. No programming was exempt from our parsing and scrutinizing, even cartoons — especially Disney — were examined for negative cultural messages, symbolism that informed the identity and ideas of my generation. I loved to play our three-step game: *1-Why this isn't true 2- What it says about you, and 3- What is true?* We traveled back in time contextualizing minstrel shows, stopping to listen to the proud alternative, the original Paul Robeson recordings that played on vinyl speed 78. It was through that exploration that I began to grasp the concept of cultural humiliation.

The word *humiliation* became one of the countless vocabulary words I received every Monday from the age of five to 13 before mom ventured out to what was sometimes two jobs.

Mother gave me the gift of loving myself through calculated lessons. At four years old, I sat on the floor poised to play. She displayed images of the blackest people I have seen to date. She explained they were my ancestors, first humans, with grand civilizations in Africa. These beautiful people were from the Sudan and they were black because of the sun and climate and their closeness to the equator, their rich pigment. She brought out a large block-colored map; we found Sudan and the equator. She almost cooed as her hands lightly passed over the treasured images. Mother was not the cooing type so I knew these people were really special, and by association so was I —Black and Beautiful. The words *ancestor* and *equator* were placed on next week's word list.

Mother James was defined by precision and exactness. She was a meticulous, disciplined creature, from the High Order of *Meticulanians*. As adults, my sister Lynn and I would tease her: "Oh, Queen Meticulous, we are your dusty subjects. May we enter beyond the Threshold of Cleanliness; we have not been sanitized, My Lady." We would bow to the Queen of Cleanliness at the door of her bedroom. Mother would wave us along telling us to get out of here with such nonsense. I believe she was secretly proud that everything was immaculate and in order.

Teachers, mother's friends, Girl Scout Leaders, my friends' parents, and adults in general made it a point to remark about my height. They would say: "You sure are tall for your age." If mother was present she would defend with a retort: "She's going to be tall like her father." Several went as far as to tell

me over and over again that I was going to be as tall as the trees, which to me suggested that I might never stop growing. As you might imagine, I was regularly teased as the tallest girl in my elementary and middle school class — before tall and lanky was a fashion statement. Maybe that's how I acquired my affinity with trees. After all, the trees stood alone and so did I.

My backyard library was above it all, up in the tree, where I read books and hung out with branches. Among the leaves, I consumed: *Things Fall Apart, Go Tell it on the Mountain, Wretched of the Earth*, and more from mother's extensive literary collection. Every night Mother dutifully read with me or my sister Lynn. One day after my decent from an exceptionally tall climb, Mother asked, "Did you see the holes in the bark? Did you notice the leaves curling?" I was about nine years old. I hadn't noticed those tiny specs on the tree's skin that looked like newly inverted pimples. She informed, "That tree is dying. We will work to save it." The tree was in full blossom, with clusters of beautiful pink and red flowers forming a canopy of glory. How could it be dying? I was beginning to learn things are not always as they appear. "We will work to save it," she said with conviction. We were always working to save someone or something.

It was post 1967 Detroit Rebellion, before the election of Coleman A, Young for Mayor of Detroit. It was a complex time for a young Black girl to comprehend.

This year was the year of the final raspberry lesson. I was twelve, junior high school bound. Mom and I were in the garden. I dug a hole for the new rose bush that bore the name, "The Doctor." That would be my special rose bush, a gift from Mother. Everything Mother did was aspirational, purposeful.

"Which is the raspberry vine and which is the sucker?" "This is the sucker;" I palmed the stem assuredly. I continued as if I were teaching a class, "It is slightly thicker than the actual raspberry stem, and the cluster of leaves are *not* budding leaves. These sucker leaf clusters will *not* blossom into flowers, and then raspberries. Also the buds on the suckers are spaced a wider distance apart."

"Yes!" Mother was ebullient. Her fist pumped the air. She added: "In life, there will be suckers and there will be vines; one is real and the other pretends to be real. It is your job to distinguish between them. You must be able to identify real people from false people. Situations that may look like they are in your best interest with further examination, may not be. You must to be able to tell the raspberry vine from the sucker, for the sucker looks real but steals all the strength from the vine that actually bears the fruit. Always remember, the sucker bears no fruit; its sole purpose is to take away nutrients from that which is real, weakening the vine. Never let anyone or anything weaken you or misuse you. You will encounter people who will be suckers, users. Know who they are and pull them out of your life just as we are going to uproot these suckers this afternoon. After we get rid of these imposters, we will have a good yield of raspberries: raspberry jam on toast or toppings on vanilla ice cream." Mom was twisting and pretending to lick her lips, and pat her tummy, acting silly.

I laughed a proud smile, and exclaimed, "I like to eat them plain, fresh picked." Mother's eyes smiled back as she handed me a sharp tool, and we began the process of uprooting those suckers.

Mother James was a complex woman of her time. Born in 1918, she was the granddaughter of the Woodson family, who escaped slavery via the Underground Railroad, and settled in Saskatchewan and later in Amherstburg, Canada. Her father, Horace, one of 22 children, left the farm in Essex County, Canada to relocate in Detroit for employment at Ford Motor Co., which offered $5 per day wages, a great deal of money for the time. Bessie L. James grew up as a Detroit West-sider, raised by her mother, Elmira, a Garveyite, and her father Horace, a union organizer. She developed into a Soldier for International Human Rights, and was the recipient of a Lifetime Appreciation Award from the Southern Poverty Law Center.

Mother James was on a mission for restoration of African culture and history. She traveled to West Africa to "go home." She was an active lifetime member of the Association for the Study of African American Life and History.

She assisted Dr. Charles H. Wright during the formative years of establishing the Museum of African American History when it was located in a house on West Grand Boulevard. My mother, also known as Mama Esi, was a vital member of the Pan-African Congress. As mother to two daughters, Jacqueline James and Semaj Brown, Mother James taught her girls programmatically. Weekends were filled with trips to theater, concerts, museums and lectures. She cultivated with fervor a passion and appreciation for world culture, class and racial struggle, socio-political literature, art, drama, dance, Black Creative Classical Music (Jazz), and opera.

A classically accomplished pianist, Mother James studied and performed European composition, and taught at the Detroit Conservatory of Music. Despite her exceptional talents, she experienced bigotry. Through much agitation and protest, along with her dear friends, Arthur Coar, Marguerite Massey and others, Bessie L. James was one of the establishing members of Friends of African Art at the Detroit Institute of Arts. For decades, Mother James extensively researched lynching in the United States. She made trips to the Schomburg Center for Research in Black Culture in Harlem and the Library of Congress. For years, her notes and papers were sprawled across the dining room table. Now they provide support material for continued research and remain a family treasure. A master gardener, lover of teatime and everything beautiful, including antiques, Mother James insisted she felt closest to God while working in her garden.

Wooing the Bubble on Boston Boulevard

Open the front door of Jeannette's home and the bellow of scatting horns speaking syncopated conversations engulfs you. Before my mind offers a greeting, I see words flying toward me in a color storm, sometimes raining orange or blazing cobalt blue. The tempos and context of these musical jaunts evoke the dreams I borrowed and long ago returned. I was peeking through the prism of history in real time. Rarely does the opportunity present to witness phenomena germinating. Before the fall, and subsequent gentrification of our beloved Detroit, there was a constant force of renewal emanating from a 19th century home on historic Boston Boulevard. If only those storied walls could talk, the narrative would rival that of the Great Gatsby, with Jeannette Murrell reimagined as the protagonist, presiding over the flurry, pomp, circumstance and revelations of art.

Living icons taller than the 15-foot ceilings encircled a dining room table, legends blowing Jazz, playing into our imaginations. They were the final generation of beboppers! These public broadcasting moments were worthy of documentation. In awe, I looked for a videographer, but there were guests only, people who would someday serve as memory. We will be the raconteurs, I thought. This transformational happening was about the enrichment of beings, and the celebration of African American art, which commented upon and carved worlds. I was there wooing the bubble, this in-between, indefinable, amorphous space where inspiration bobs and weaves a wobble of influence over the expression of my cultural aesthetic. The bubble is translucent; a gossamer sheath of floating spirit, an ephemeral cloud where my poetic muses rested and rose like a wave from the after death of birth. The three muses, Khalil Gibran, Rumi, and Pablo Neruda, were passengers in this buoyant, bouncing bubble of mine. These bygone literary sages inspired the poems found in this collection. "Purified Ganges River Man" is a writing that calls to us from both the Nile and the Detroit River, from circa 1942 and 4,500 years ago. "What If, Then" is a poem whose imaginings caravan through incarnations to at last find me to use as conduit. Gibran, Rumi and Neruda were consummate companions for a seven-year stretch— intensifying my life, a life that was perpetually hemorrhaging, bleeding fire; they offered poetry as a gift, and as a tourniquet.

The atmosphere at Jeannette's was hot. Snatches of sweaty metaphor blew in obtuse melodies like ruffled hems quivering in the warm wind from the electric fan that sat outside the kitchen. Poetic ideas lay sweltering in the cut of rhythm to be interpreted later. Some ideas were bold; they promenaded about like birds in a rainforest courtship, showing off their feathers, exposing their colors. The deep purple of a longing verse was embroidered upholstery. An inscribed pillow tried to woo me to the corner seat on the sofa to write the lines down. A cluster of lyrics circled, swarming the ceiling fan until I was dizzy. My muses gestured from the bubble I wooed and that wooed me. During their next rotation, on my tiptoes, I stretched, jumped and clasped a grouping of alphabets; it was like catching a butterfly. In my hand, the words dissolved, melted into the poem, "Light Spectrum," which appears in the Flames and Flares section of this book.

Open the side door, enter an emporium, a funhouse of abstracted landscapes designed to bend the brain. Here five iconic visual artists' exhibitions crawled sideways up three flights that seemed to provide a staircase to the outer limits. The soundscape was a respectful murmur as admiring converts mulled about, discussing technique, the sublime, and whatever came to the mind of this intergenerational, multi-ethnic collective of intelligentsia and ordinary folk. I watched a little girl follow the vertical lines of an acrylic painting, her small head tilting backwards, eyelids lifting. I asked what she thought. She replied, "It's beautiful, I am going to live in there," pointing to a part of the painting that resembled a red cloud. She, too, was wooing the bubble, being primed for creative explosion.

In Jeanette Murrell's real life, ongoing art community novel, all who care to have access to art should have access, including those who do not yet realize art's medicinal benefits. For 25 years, visiting artists have sculpted dreams in the form of art installations, film, ironwork, and blown glass poetry on the grounds of her extraordinary home. They worked in spaces infused with the scent of wild mint and the sounds of fresh, unfamiliar languages. As an educator who thrills in the sphere of innovation, I am grateful to have had the distinct privilege of periodically drawing inspiration from and contributing to this unique collage of human artistry so cultivated by the bubble Ms. Murrell woos.

Cass Tech (Fish Eyes)

*(Cass Technical High School, founded 1907, is a four-year
university preparatory high school in Detroit, Michigan. Thank you
Amie Whitaker Osborne for requesting I pen a poem about Cass Tech
for our 40th Class Reunion.)*

I

It was invisible, invisible,
but my 14-year-old *Funkenstein imagination could
see it through these prophetic fish eyes.

This imperceptible monstrosity— "this thing"
locking gears in the vacant lot lagoon on E. 7 Mile and Ryan
across from Pershing High was

invisible, invisible but

I could see its ghost-like outline through murky urban waters.
"This thing/this it"

Translucent monster- killing machine with Medusa-like
appendages snatched that boy

Leonard who lived two blocks down, you know Leonard
fed him to some unnamed, out-of-sight entity.

My 14-year-old self told me,

"this thing/ this it"

MUST be

Deployed to disintegrate bricks
implode interiors of my neighborhood schools

Deployed on a sea of cement
amphibious assault missiles sent
 to fish out a name to call itself 4 decades later
a name like school-to-prison pipeline
a name like mass incarceration.

But in 1974,

"this thing /this it"

remained phantom anonymous
only my 14-year-old prophetic fish eyes could see.

AND FEEL

The grind, uh huh, pulverizing asphalt to gravel
Mechanized nets of capture, containment
The grind, uh huh, lowered, unhinged
across the expanse of 313 area code

It was invisible, invisible,
but I could hear the grind, uh huh, reverberations
whiplashing as "IT"
 confiscated banks and propped up check cashing fronts

as "IT" held hostage small businesses and shoe repair to
the ravages of clown painted pink and orange
liquor stores, liquor stores, liquor stores

as "IT" discharged nuclear annihilation of groceries
 to the propagation of fast food desserts.

"This thing/this it"
This invisible, invisible
I could sense

despite the jubilation of newly elected
Coleman A. Young
and eradication of DPD Stress Terror Unit

I could feel
undercurrent rumbling of Detroit River surging my veins
warning me, telling me

"Make like a salmon with imprinted mission and
swim the *Aqua Boogie!"

II

So I did what any
magical-thinking, violin-playing, natural-hair-wearing,
P Funk convert, 14-year-old prophetic fish-eyed girl would
do.

I dove: *Psycho alpha disco beta bio aqua doloop

into the fire of the Woodward Canal, my fro a fin-shaped blaze
southbound hydroplaning to Second Avenue
final watering hole of intellectual rigor—
Cass Technical High School!

The Green and White Oasis — teeming with Technicians
throngs of wide-eyed prophetic neon-lit fishes just like me.

Streamlining, genuflecting to the spawning of knowledge
and mutating the ethnic cleansing legacy of its namesake.

The radioactive re-generating generation had arrived rocking
that 78

After the 67 Rebellion
decades before Black Lives Matter
the in-between re-generating generation
exhaled optimism of Dubois talented tenth pre-tuned
to *Atomic dog bow wow wow yippee yo hipee haw

For 4 years
solar flares dropped from the Mothership
guiding the pilgrims sojourn,
awash in *flash light, and
red light and
neon light and
stop light.

They swam from relative privilege, relative ghettos

back and forth stroking in automobiles —snow
surfing atop 1, 2, 3, ice-covered coaches
treading in bus terminals to transfer

books into our brains
smooch test tubes into our ears.

we transformed into paint brushes
turned into runway textiles turned into Polar Bears
a cappella calculus
grew syncopated eight notes
into symphonies, into guitar strings
danced chemical metallurgy
in back hall performing arts Bio
distributive education
computer programming aerospace flying
business administration defining
a health and welfare state in a
heat-fixed thought cauldron of Science and Art.

We helped *Sir Nose overcome his fear of swimming while
drafting and constructing our architectural futures!

III

Cass Tech! Cass Tech! Cass Technicians align like planetary
systems and
combust into a Radiant Ring
CT Galaxy of Re-generating generation 78 Energy as One
Nation under a ...

Now CT social workers, educators, ministers are

are reclaiming our remnants, rebuilding the fragments

of re-constituted people
from the dust and debris
from the cultural apocalypse fall out from

"that thing/ that it"
that happened to our beloved Motown, our beloved Detroit.

IV

Those Green and White Technician star fishes imbued
with neural plasticity grew legs and
climbed that corporate ladder and then decided to
grow wings and
flew from that corporate ladder
CT became a mogul, a microphone, medicine
best employees of companies
became the company

and got married or didn't
got unmarried or didn't

had children or didn't
loss children or didn't

came out or didn't
went in or didn't

and got really, really, really sick or didn't and
got really, really, really well or didn't

and joined the green and white striped
butterfly technician Ancestor Angels transmitting
blessings from the Cosmos.

Cass Tech rocking that 78 became a Sports Force
the military, journalists, activists
exemplary officer of the state
became the state
became a brief, a deposition,
THE LAW, became a POET and
 *Tore the roof off the sucker, TORE THE ROOF OFF
THE SUCKER,
 TORE THE ROOF OFF THE SUCKER of lofty academia!

V

And like homing birds circling their electrified destiny or
Haley's Comet astral shooting its return

We are the Green and White Serengeti Star Migration
One Nation Under a …

We are that radioactive re-generating generation
who pledged allegiance to the *F-u-n-k;
 Can you dig it?

We are electromagnetic elephants gathering, HERE,

at the Charles H. Wright watering hole to drink in 3D and

say: I see you, I see you, I remember you, I know you,
good to meet you! I love you! Thank you for affirming my
existence!

Cass Tech! Class of 1978 Forty Year Reunion! Funkateers
forever!

----

*All asterisks in this poem reference the copyrighted work of Parliament
Funkadelics/ George Clinton.*

Be Winged!

(Dedicated to Flint Chapter Pierians, The Pierians, Inc., and The Pierian Foundation.
The Pierians is an arts appreciation organization dedicated to promoting and studying fine arts.)

Pierians airbrush the world with poetry. They are clay molders shaping a future for children and community. Pierians speak music to the wind. They breathe promise. These are women who mine beauty where so much is ugly.

So who are the Pierians? They are:

Flamingo Moon Dancers

Carving Mud Molders

Glassblowing Torch Enchanters

Hitchcock Wood Whittlers

Creative Sleeping Virtuosos

Buried Man in Nuclear Sand Castle-ers

Shakespearean Bluegrass Sassafras

Green Haired Tea Takers

One-Eyed Humped-Back Filmmakers

They are: graphic designing Monkey Signifying

Passive aggressive mimes

Possessed puppeteers

Origami Engineers

They make: Weaponry Photography

They be: Graffiti brush stroking ballet leapers

Drum Reed tree String strung Players

Choral Crooners and Subversive Comedic Buffoon-ers

They are: deep beat boxers Julliard drop out-ers

Fashion incarcerators and

Culinary Satiate-tors

To Cosmetic Make up Make down
demolition Transformers

To the Clinched Fist Dramatists

To electro technos

To blood diamond ice sculptures

Installation-ists

Lighting technicians shadow banishers

Horticultural beautification-ists

Delta blues pluckin' it wash tub sayin' it

Who are the Pierians?

———————————————

The poem, "Be Winged!" was inspired by Free Flow, an acrylic painting rendered by Dr. James Brown.

Pearl Formation

(Dedicated to the Zeta Phi Beta Sorority, Incorporated founded on January 16, 1920, at Howard University by five women who are referred to as The Five Pearls.
Renowned authors, Zora Neal Hurston and Gwendolyn Brooks, were members.)

From enslavement ships to scholarship
From servitude to service
From hood to sisterhood
From wounded women to finer women with purpose
From sand to land to Pearls who command

Born in the terminal bend of century
into a swashing cauldron of upheaval
founders of Zeta Phi Beta Sorority, Incorporated:
Arizona Cleaver Stemons
Myrtle Tyler Faithful
Fannie Pettie Watts
Viola Tyler Goings
Pearl Anna Neal
labored post-Civil War spasms only
35 years earlier they
would have been property but

Time, time regurgitated
the vile consumption of slavery and

Time, time given funeral to Reconstruction

(10-year period 1865-1877)
when Black folks voted
became Congressmen and gentry friend
entrepreneurs and Connoisseurs
yes that time, time of Reconstruction was dead dead
19th century promises shredded
promises buried with the curling skeleton of Jim Crow head
20th century shone like a diabolical 2-faced moon
Harlem Renaissance shining as
dank shadows of discrimination —grinding
Terror Reign over 4, 000 lynchings had begun
aspirations hung, unsung
Time—Time—of yearning
Time, time of burr-nn-ing

From enslavement ships to scholarship
From servitude to service
From hood to sisterhood
From wounded women to finer women with purpose
From sand to land to Pearls who command

Our founders came of age in
communities that convulsed from
seas of raging racism
violent waves heaved tossing
Black women from kitchen to field
plant or be planted
share croppin' in
a nation clamshell shut to Negroes but
self-determined double X chromosome dynamism
dislodged sand bank barriers of unrighteous denial

excavated truth from decomposed sediments and
one Grain of Sand navigated under tow traveling from
Missouri and
one Grain of Sand traversed hostile waters from Georgia
yet another Grain from North Carolina
barreled forward with unwavering stroke and
two Grains of Sand survived thrashing rapids of River Ohio
crossing turbulent currents of 1920

Time — 1920 grew and swelled
the malignant incarceration of Black men until
splitting veins of bondage by another name called
chain gang labor built
the industrial multi-national corporations of today

Time — 1921 Black Wall Street Tulsa Oklahoma Greenwood
affluent neighborhoods — bombed!
5,000 mothers fathers grandparents aunties uncles nephews,
nieces babies — eviscerated, massacred
hospitals, schools, colleges, airports, businesses, bus systems,
millions of dollars, all Black, all Black, all Black, all gone!

So Time, time — 1920 scaling the crooked spine of liberty
against forces of hostile gravity
swimming the northern ladder up South
clawing a quest for higher education — were
acts of Rebellion!

The founders of Zeta Phi Beta Sorority, Incorporated were
the coiffeur hair

hat-donning
white glove-wearing
poised and polished fearless
revolutionaries of their time.
They powered a courageous resistance.

From enslavement ships to scholarship
From servitude to service
From hood to sisterhood
From wounded women to finer women with purpose
From sand to land to Pearls who command

Time — in 2006, the largest pearl was discovered
off the Philippine coast weighing 75 pounds
sold for 100 million dollars

Pearl the only jewel formed
inside an animal, a mollusk
also, apparently, formed inside the belly of a seething society
a society clamshell shut to Black women in 1920

But those freedom seeking Grains of Sand
crossed that impenetrably hard clamshell and
found a more hospitable soft tissue
found a womb inside Howard University and
there in the soft tissue, in the womb of Howard U
Sand did what sand will do when turning itself into a pearl

Sand became an irritant at Mecca U
grating deep below the cuticle of injustice
carving a century-long intellectual path
Sand became an irritant
sand-papering indignities

redeeming honor of their foremothers' stolen virtue and
razor rubbed until norms of 2nd class citizenry were chafe

Sand became a dangerous irritant
irritant to the status quo that had to go!
Sand agitated and dug out and dug up
lifted and organized and strategized and
fashioned weaponry from trigonometry and music theory and
Sand became educators and Sand became social workers and
administrators and leaders
The clamshell shut society tried to protect itself
from this dangerous irritant and so secreted nacre
a material intended for obstruction but
Sand utilized nacre for self-creation!

Nacre — material hard as clamshell calcium carbonite
designed to isolate, surrounded and submerged sand,
contained sand, covered sand, walled-off sand while
turning, churning, layering nacre, time layering nacre
the glistening glow of unbreakable nacre
hardened in the glimmering soft tissue womb of Howard U
smoothing, smoothing, filing, compacting,
compressing making stronger and finer crystalizing
through gestation, self-creation formation until

Time, time — five Grains of Sand transformed — rebirthed as

five glorious, luminous victorious Pearls

founders of Zeta Phi Beta Sorority, Incorporated!

From enslavement ships to scholarship
From servitude to service
From hood to sisterhood
From wounded women to finer women with purpose
From sand to land to
Pearl Champions!
Pearl Champions!
Pearl Champions!

The Call of the Purified Ganges River Man
(For Faruq Z. Bey)

You Call Back
from 4,500 years of coma
from the trance of frozen grapes
from sketches of Spain, a Moorish model

Purified Ganges River Man
You call back from Mahogany Cafes to a net
where it is safe to remember temple Luxor
where *Metu-netr* monuments are organically mined
where you tread
through pools of hemorrhaging vision

Abdullah Faithful Servant Man
You prostrating while fiends stomped prayers
sterilizing sisters circa 1942 Eugenics poison
their bodies floated fluid less and bleached
all to kill to the memory of God
but the memory remains in the carcass of truth
but the memory remains in the call to Dogon ancestors
but the memory remains
to mend the genes of this razor walking sister
the genes they tried to sear into a million poly parts

Watershed of Justice Man
You call back East five times a day
to prayers (duas and salat)
You could have been my sheik

This is ancient sampling with Be Bop tongue
You could have been my sheik
calling me out of this phantom millennium
to a time when sound shouldered quantities of salt
and became sea to time when *Know Thyself* was
itched in eternity
to time of limestone and quartz of talking igneous
in the souls of metamorphic Cats

Voyeur of Wavelength Frequency Theory Man
You call us back on Monday nights
from the yellow light in Bomac's Blues and Jazz parking lot
We listen with whole bodies
livers, kidneys, spleens grow eardrums
that beat beat beat a
syncopated Oh Yeah!
You call us back back front to the science of entropy
the 2nd Law of Thermodynamics
challenging our *Tendency toward Disorder*
to truth of Albert Ayler's bells vibrating from
the throats of caged birds

Brother Seeking Ginkgo Biloba Man
Thank you for searching the diaspora for our lost names
for evoking the sting
an undeniable salute to peace
for confirming our existence in a mirage of past paradise
This is ancient sampling with Bebop tongue

Ascending Humanity in Linear Spine Man
You call us back to rivers: silt of the Nile,
soot of Detroit
You call us to shoe-less wave dancing
to the medicine of horehound candy
to Aretha albums
to recipes of piccolo
and spirit

Fire Weaver

(For Dr. Karen Weaver, Mayor of Flint, Michigan)

On Ogun's land
On Ogun's land
West Afrikan Alkebulan

Ancestors forged iron by hand
Flint descendants forged steel for automobile
The connection is unbroken
The spirit is real

Before the Trans-Atlantic Slave Trade
before the Middle Passage made
before Holocaust of Black People
before Christ, before steeple

ancient Africans were imbued with philosophy
antiquity was the birthplace of science and technology
Adorned in robes of gold and silk
brushed in myrrh and frankincense
with gele headdresses wrapped high
to kiss the mountain sky
igniting heavens, oh yes, they could fly!
these were the Fire Keepers
They were the Future Seers

Elders sat in the round
around the flickering pit
and read the curling heat of the futuristic script

They read and spoke in hushed tongues
in the language of prophecy
about the baby who would come
born as a ball of light
in a Mid-Western City

The Elders read:

The light will grow plaits that swing from her head
The light will have a moonbeam smile
The light will develop a brain that recycles fire from rain
and there will be peace for a while

The Elders said:

The people will call the light Karen
The people will call the light Doctor
The people will call the light Mayor
And we the Elders, the Seers of Light
will call her by her anointed name
one who makes fire from the rain

On Ogun's land
On Ogun's land
West Afrikan Alkebulan

Ancestors forged iron by hand
Flint descendants forged steel for automobile
The connection is unbroken
The spirit is real

Sooooooooo when the dark time came
and the beautiful people of Flint were maimed
folks cried out!
Lies! Lies like snakes slivered all about
The light throughout the land receded
the Fire Weaver was called
to make her light tall
And the Fire Weaver plucked a thread of lightning
and the Fire Weaver snatched a spindle of flame
She knitted a net of burrrning power
making fire from the rain
The Fire Weaver makes fire from rain!

The Awakening

In memory of my beloved daughter, Robyn Sampson (1993-2000)

"Mommy, that's a poem! That's a poem!" My almost four-year-old daughter was referring to the words she had just uttered while poking me in my side, breaking into my 3:00 a.m. stream of consciousness writing. Tonight we were sharing my bed and Robyn had just awakened from a heavily medicated sleep. I was thrilled that she appeared to be feeling substantially better. She sat propped against a pillow, speaking the most poignant and haunting verses that seemed to be transported from the twilight of her dreams. Together, wide-eyed, we spied the alarm clock, counting the hours before she could call yet another enthusiastic listener, grandma. For Robyn, poetry had become medicine, the real antidote. When this little girl wrote, it was like inscribing sunbeams into her long days of dark suffering, which she endured due to sickle cell disease.

One Sunday afternoon, while in attendance at Broadside Press Poet's Theatre, we watched as the clipboard for open mic circulated throughout the room, bobbing from hand to hand like an unattended raft. Robyn harpooned the opportunity, signing her name in a giant cursive scrawl on line number five of the sign-up sheet. The conversation that would ensue between daughter and mother in the next few moments would be awkwardly wedged between rows of metal folding chairs. I was crouched down in a narrow aisle trying to convince my determined offspring that this was not an ideal time for her first public reading. I noted how important preparation was and that she had not practiced. I even questioned whether she had a poem fully memorized. Finally, I insisted that the bright lights of Channel 56 (they were recording a special) might make her nervous.

Robyn politely countered my every worry with a litany of buts, while Willie Williams, the director of Broadside Press Poet's Theatre, stood anchored close by, supporting Robyn, as was his way with all the participating writers. Yes, his miniature student of poetry was indeed encouraged and quite inspired. "Five, four, three," our exchange was interrupted by the countdown of the public television director. My argument was out of time. I conceded. The film began to roll.

With a defined intensity, Robyn eased back into her chair. Her tiny hands were clasped tightly in her lap while her short legs dangled two t-strapped black leather shoes. Though she stared steely, straight ahead, there seemed to be an impish smile just below the surface of her severe expression. When they called her name, she sprang up and bounced down to the stage area so quickly that my heart missed the traditional opportunity to drop. Instead, I held my breath. The audience was adjusting themselves, shifting their chairs to look over and down at this very small child. The microphone stand had been lowered all the way, yet it still towered above her head. The lights were glaring. The room was a captive hush amplified by the anticipation of the onlookers.

Robyn broke open the silence with the conviction of a serious artist. First, she began by stating the title of her two-stanza poem. When she proceeded to speak, her words formed a conveyor belt of meaning that extended from her mouth to the hearts of the listeners. She concluded her recitation with a bow followed by a princess curtsy. The cheering erupted into a rain of proud applause. Happily, she returned to her seat, plopping down beside me in a sea of whispered questions: "Who is that little girl?" "Did she write that?" "How old is she?"

Of course, I was a very proud mother who had learned a valuable lesson from that experience; but what was even more rewarding was to know that the confidence and self-esteem that my daughter exhibited had been instilled in hundreds of children who participated in the Poet-in-Residence Program over the past ten years. The poet / facilitators working in this program helped to cultivate what was innate, but too often left dormant in the individual. Self-expression, human need, was molded into the meaningful art from of poetry during a decade of work shopping.

Through such classes many children and adults who would not have otherwise given voice to their silent thoughts have developed the poetic consciousness so necessary in these times.

Reprinted from Poet in the House: The Poet in Residence Program: A Decade of Collaboration between Broadside Poets and the Detroit Public Library Copyright 2005 Broadside Press, Detroit.

Is That Really Poetry?

She said, "I hate poetry, but I love your work."
Sandra Walker, 2019

Sandra, a brilliant woman and lifelong friend, is one of many
beautiful people who declare their fervent disdain for the
genre of poetry while heaping praise upon my poems. I find
this a bit disconcerting. Last summer, I was invited to read my
creation love poem, "Remember Re mem ber ing," at a dear
friend's wedding. An enthusiastic young man, a millennial
spoken word artist, approached me: "I never heard poetry like
this. Is it really poetry?" Smiling, I affirmed, "It's poetry." His
eyes communicated earnest disbelief; his eyes moved as if
searching for something hidden. "It can't be poetry," he
protested. "I don't know what you call it, but I never heard
any poetry like this. It's fire though, it's fire!" Many variations
of this scenario have played out over time. They are surreal
moments when what is popularly thought of as poetry and
what I write converge, staring me down like a dare.

I venture that the reticence or confusion many people feel
about poetry may have been fostered during their elementary
school years, when Robert Frost and Emily Dickerson were
elevated as the only viable standard of American verse. That
was certainly the way of my elementary school education, but
I was equipped with a secret: my mother's ultraviolet
teachings, to supplant, augment, and circumvent my state-
sponsored inferior education, particularly in the area of
literature. It is also possible that this quandary about what
constitutes as poetry may be due to popular writing styles.

Most of my work does not reflect the end phrase rhyming lilt of coffee house poets and finger snappers, or the driving 4/4 meter, which is standard among many contemporary shock spoken word performers — though I attempted to write in the former, and succeeded in achieving the latter. Let me suggest, with humor, that the answer may be found in Volume Two of *Poetry Suppression, Academia, and the Rise of Popular Culture* — a study I have yet to undertake!

Writing *Bleeding Fire! Tap the Eternal Spring of Regenerative Light* has forced my focus inward, toward the examination of my methods and influences. It has been an unexpected period of discovery. Secrets and clues to processes are emerging that may address the poetry/not poetry conundrum. I will share with you what is revealed to me, as we are in this together. After all, these poems, or whatever you choose to call them, are written for your eyes, your ears, and your heart.

"Finally I was able to see that if I had a contribution to make,

I must do it, despite what others said. That I was OK the way I was. That it was alright to be strong."

Wangari Maathai

Conflagrations and Transgressions (Me Too)

Concerning Conflagrations and Transgressions (Me Too)

Tarana Burke is the African-American civil rights activist who founded of the *Me Too* movement in 2006. Originally, *Me Too* was an advocacy campaign for women of color against sexual assault and violence. The phrase *Me Too* engenders empathy and empowerment. Ms. Burke was born September 12, 1973 in Bronx, NY. In 2017, Burke and other influential women activists were named "the silence breakers" by *Time* magazine.

The poems in this *Me Too* section speak to the atrocious statistics concerning sexual abuse and sexual assault of girls and women. Many of us are victims. According to the Rape, Abuse, Incest, National Network (RAINN), the nation's largest organization against sexual violence, every 90 seconds a person is sexually assaulted in the United States. Seventy percent of sexual assaults victimize children 17 years of age and younger. Ninety-three percent of children sexually abused know their abuser. One in four girls is sexually abused before age 18. For help or information Call National Sexual Assault Hotline: 800. 656. HOPE (4673)

Girls are unsafe in our society. Child abuse is a global disgrace; it is big business. Poems in this section speak to the great conflagration, the enormous all-consuming burning that destroys an entire forest or an entire person, family, community, or society as a result of the flagrant abuse of girls and women predominately perpetrated by men.

Misogyny is the hatred of women. Misogynistic transgressions transpire on a moral level as high crimes against humanity. Many who have survived these deviant tragedies exist as fractions of the person they might have been as they struggle with physical and psychological damage for a lifetime. Statistics indicate sexually abused girls often grow into women who are at risk for violence, rape, addiction, incarceration, mental illness, and prostitution.

And yet there are those resilient women, who while gagging on the sewerage of abuse, siphon courage from the *eternal spring of regenerative light* and blaze brighter, beyond conflagration of violation. Through the miraculous process of spiritual healing, and by accessing professional services and mentorship programs, these women are able to extinguish, redirect and transmute pain into the energy of repair and triumph.

ROAR (Rhymes of Applied Rights)

These rhymes are boundary-building affirmations to be used while stepping, cheering, jumping rope or singing camp songs, or during Rites of Passage — or anytime to reinforce a girl's or a woman's ROAR.

ROAR (Rhymes of Applied Rights)

I

A, B, C, Don't touch me
4, 5, 6, None of your tricks
7, 8, 9 If I say no
Don't cross the line

II

I imitate no one
I am the sole one
I am unique
If you can't see me
Then, you can't see
Glasses are what you need

III

No, means, hell no!
I don't care, if you go
In fact, I will leave
I can do as I please
because
I am free, free, free!

IV

I'm not honey
I'm not sticky
Just call me by my name
Respect will come more quickly

V

Violence against me
You should dread
Tables have turned
I'll leave you for dead

VI

My body is my body
My hair is my hair
My vulva is my vulva
Don't you put your hands there!

VII

My chest will grow breasts
Not to push up and expose
Why must I be the one to dance
half naked without clothes?

VIII

I don't want to have children
Till I want to have children
If I want to have children, okay
Preconditioning,
preprogramming
not here, not now
will have its way!

I don't want to have a baby
Till it's time to have a baby
And it won't be time, till I say
Till I make up my mind
Cause my mind
is *my* mind,
is *my* Mind,
is *my* Mind
I slay

IX

Beauty is a gift
Given at birth
Your compliments
Your approval
don't give me value or worth

X

I am legitimate because I exist
I am valuable, the ancestor's gift
I am worthy, a girl who will build
a better world for families
to live fulfilled

XI

Because I like you
And you like me
You don't own me
I'm not your property

Must We, Really?

Must you really stab darts at my venomous tongue?

Must we grovel to the level of sparring boar pigs?

Must my face rubber band from thrashing slaps?

Must you strangle my ankles and
use my hair as chimney sweep?

Must my earlobes be cutters of glass windows?

Must my body be pretzel twisted?

Must you disregard the laws of aeronautics
crash sailing me over furniture dreams?

Must we vie for the championship of the 32nd round?

Must time out be a chaotic rematch?

Must you kiss with artillery in your taste buds?

Must I camouflage our home with jungle prints
for war time fall out maneuvers?

Or

Should I play dead and pray the enemy comes to rescue me?

These Needy Men

The takers, the needers, the true whores
those who prostitute life, engulfing and devouring
all along their way
leaving residue paths lined with decayed lovers,
dregs insoluble to life

The needers, you needy men, always taking, wanting
everything, even my underwear
That I wondered about

Auctioning mobility what was stationary you did not respect
leaving me open to other vandals like yourself

Needy man, in your lusty thirst gazed hungrily
upon my mammaries
while I screamed
"These breasts aren't lactating this milk unformed
is for my children unborn."

Needy man, such mastery you display
in pretense of sweet sensual love making
sent tubes soaring up my vagina
in search of eggs to enhance your breakfast

Needy man, you are a needy man of course with just cause:
a strong mother, a weak mother, a female fault
The village people became your favorite entertainers
when they sang "Macho Man"
because every woman wants a brutal, I mean macho man

The needers, you needy men, always taking, wanting
everything, even my fingernails
That I wondered about

Carefully place belongings periodically disappeared
My toenails processed for cherry gelatin
My pubic hair compiled into miniature wigs
for 12-inch fashion dolls
Mass production of silicon leaking, poison secreting,
toxic buts—
for your pleasure to watch me strut

Needy man, have you no heart?
Inventory reveals your museum of waxed cardiacs
synchronizing heartbeats sustaining your strength

Needy man, you are a greedy man, a vampire of sorts
perking pumped blood for coffee
rationalizing con artistry one afternoon said you loved me

That I wondered about!

I Will

After you drive your truck through me
I will not settle like dust on a road

I will not

be a bioengineering experiment
my dummy head crashing the windshield of European cars

I will not

Be turned into a future find for archaeologists
students pondering the holes in my fossilized cranium

I will not

Shrink into a bowl of scarlet sauce
and pretend that it is not my blood

I will not

Forgive you for grinding the skeleton of small boned women

I will not

Play Billy Holidays' "Good Morning, Heartache"

I will not

Be patient as the prayer plant that awaits the shine of justice

I will not

Carry the pain of exaggeration in a papoose of bitterness

I will not

Sacrifice one regret when the spirit of Queen Nzinga
rises in me and I ride on the back of a winged Black Panther
across town to your favorite bar

I will not

Hesitate or quiver when your face turns from comedy to
tragedy
and you realize the taste of ale is your last supper

I will not settle peacefully like dust on a road
after you have driven your truck through me

I will not

Forbidden Flora

Flora's petals are poems not to be fondled
       she has budded swelling cocoa roses
A dewy transgression of silken kisses were
secrets zipped into her cleaving florets.

Secrets that crawled over her adornments like
aberrant butterflies burrowing
for nectar
festering.

Secrets that mutated into buzzing territorial wasp,
       stinging.

Secrets that became the seducing African bees of daydreams
swarming in the throat of her recollections

Wings flapping like the intended tongue
of an immature lover

Secrets rotting into hives like heart barracks

---

*The poem, "Forbidden Flora," was inspired after looking into Flora,
an acrylic painting rendered by Dr. James Brown.*

Other Monsters

At first I thought, all this drama —
why he's imitating Godzilla. How retro!
 You know, Godzilla that prehistoric sea monster
that ransacks the model city on
the big screen, and captured the
helpless damsel probably that
same pathetic woman who
kept falling down during the 1950s
graveyard scene when Dracula was
chasing her. Then I thought, I'll need a
stunt woman to replace me in this one.
His anger was a tornado over turning
ottomans, chairs, lamps, and the like.

I remember the wisdom of the Bayou Cypress
speaking through the voice of a centenarian.
Mother Mattie raised her arms for emphasis.
Her fingers looked like bent brown twigs.
She spoke, "Study war, then get married."

After nuptials,
I boarded a flight with BMR and Associates.
Captain Madallthetime assured me that
special craft had over 400 years
of flying experience. "Remember," he said,
"BMR and Associates, a.k.a. Black Male Rage and

Other Monsters, guarantees a flight filled with
free-floating anger.
No other airline packages blame in burgers between
rye, wheat and white.

2.5 children, triple work schedules, Dracula and bloodletting,
we resided in a colonial coffin,
 a vat of pressure.
I needed a sabbatical;
he needed America to be different.
I needed marsupials to stop flying;
he needed to drive the stake through
the heart of a Tasmanian devil.
I needed Transylvania not to be in my basement;
he needed Dr. Jekyll to ascend like a rooted sprout.
I needed to smother Mr. Hyde like a mother
convicted of postpartum depression.

Captain Madallthe time directed our attention
to the left.
We were cruising atop the swamp land of Louisiana.
Since this was the rainy season,
we might be able to sight the creature
from the black lagoons.
Shocking discovery:
It was my husband sitting at our kitchen table,
dressed in a suit and tie, employable fatigues,
gulping the last bit of Joe,
ready to fight the good fight.

Imagine: American troops dug under and covered down.
Their enemy attacks, shelling is heavy.
Self-ejected from their hiding holes, the soldiers return fire,
and in an absurd twist of Hari Kari,
Brigade A aim their automatics at their comrades, Brigade B,
giving new meaning to the phrase "friendly fire."
The wife, the mother of his child, retreats from the kitchen
to the dining room using the china cabinet
as her blockade, and the wife, the mother of his child
is screaming:
"I'm on our side, Noooooo! STOP! Wait!!! She's hit!

Yaahwoool!

Yaaahwoool!

Yaahwooo!

The absence of a full moon was making me nervous.
The primal call was being piped through
the vents of the plane. Mood music perhaps?

Before matrimony, I really did not know
of his ancestry to werewolves and
lineage to dingo dogs.
The exaggerated canines, the truncated incisors,
the tracking devices, the urinating all over the house
should have tipped me off.

It was more than turbulence.
The plane was breaking in two,
an emergency exit exploded.
The wind formed knuckles that
knocked screams beyond the fiery sky.
We were spiraling perpendicular;
the crash was an inevitable metaphor;
panic was suspended in molecules of depleted oxygen.
The remaining nanoseconds left me clutching my floatation
device, and feeling much like the bride of Frankenstein.

The Spinning of an American Woman

In the eye of a hurricane you spin on your head
At 26 you buy oils slather under Maxomax make-up
to ward off that wrinkle you fear will
walk up and sit on your nose

You spin on your head and commiserate
your ancestry to Eve
You ponder Immaculate Conception
and toddle between guilt and innocence

A self- loathing centrifuge
you spin on your head until your skull is flat
until your fallopian tubes collapse

You rotate between Jezebel and Madonna
You either wear your jeans tight or you don't
You either mask your breasts with tape or
pin them on the outside of your sweater

Spinning to lose weight for summer to don a bathing suit
for that envied stroll down a pageant runway
with threads from girdles and self- help magazines
You spin in aerobics class to express your sexuality
An upside down swivel you spin on your head
until you cranium is flat
your fallopian tubes collapse

And you dream

Of snow white and the seven face lifts
of being kidnaped by an Arabian horse
of hovering billboards and Brook Shields
of amphibians bouncing heavily upon you father's lap

Some man will marry you stamp you USDA APROVED
and you'll raise your daughter to hate herself
the way mothers love their sons

"Like slavery and apartheid, poverty is not natural. It is man-made and it can be overcome and eradicated by the action of human beings."
"Overcoming poverty is not a gesture of charity."

Nelson Mandela

Radioactivity

Relating to Radioactivity

The scientific definition of a radioactive atom is one that spontaneously emits energetic particles or waves known as radiation. This radiation is emitted when an unstable nucleus transforms to some other nucleus or energy level. Thus, radiation is the primary cause of safety concerns related to nuclear energy.

A radioactive society is one comprised of unstable practices such as racism, sexism, ageism, and classism. These factors generate physical, psychological, and economic ghettos. The nuclei/ghettos emit resistant energy/activism, waves of radiation that is toxic to the stability of the state, even as the atom is transforming to another level, a fairer or more just, stable society.

The writings in this section, *Radioactivity,* concern the volatility of a society built on unstable oppressive structures, which, like a radio-reactive atom, threatens to blow up or melt down. The poem, "Hey, Big Man," speaks to the violent forces such as over policing and mass incarceration which is imposed on a people to try to minimize their resistance. The operatic work, "Freedom Tree Song," propels citizens to shift to higher levels of consciousness, and create a new state by aligning with the *eternal spring of regenerative light*, which can be interpreted in this poem as Nature.

This section begins with the poem, "The Stolen Cocoa Bean Head," which metaphorically details the making of a people into a commodity. The poem ends with a hopeful recognition that, despite the vile denaturing process, our authentic selves survive.

Almost Majnun

(Dedicated to the missing children of war, United Nations Day, 2002.
The word majnun means mad or crazy.)

I am almost *majnun* — *majnun*
>> searching for you in the cinders of cement
>>> in the limp of wounded pigeon.
Rat fowl of urban rot
Have you seen my daughter?
Are you pecking her remains from hardened asphalt?
I am lost without her.
Her lungs were my lungs were my throat in my eye.
Have you seen my daughter?
She disintegrated into a sky burial of trade.

I am almost *majnun* — *majnun*
>> detonated propellers spiral into my cabin
>> exhaust roars raining flesh
>> gray human paste covers Manhattan.
This puddle is my husband.
He was renamed the falling man.
He has joined the blood river of twisted carcass.
 I am almost *majnun* — *majnun*

Have you seen my sister?
She was tortured by a regime that looks like you
>> Lacerated in the spin of piano wire,
>> she is bleeding oil
>> a lily pad sinking in the Mediterranean.

Have you seen him?
You did see him, your brother.
You swallowed him in the gasp of television.
He is branded to the inside of your eyelids.
Descending in the blink of horror, he lives in you.
He is a tear gland squatter
        a perpetual spiral down a landscape sclera.

The Fallen Man is
falling through the broken smoke of a fireman's net
falling down the chimney of swine and coriander
falling up my nostrils into the mushroom stench of
Hiroshima and Nagasaki
falling across consciousness spinning
toward the grinding mouth of denial
falling beneath the choke hold of profiling snipers
falling over hallucinations of them falling
over hallucinations of me falling
beyond the debris of ethnic sterilization
I am skinless and blue — almost *majnun*.

Have you seen my daughter?
I am lost without her.
Her picture hangs from my neck like a stethoscope.
Her eyes are of Christ, jeweled mocha orbs.
I am looking for her in the dusk flake of air,
        in the incidental pauses between words.
A morphine drip pats time silent.

I am looking for her in the dehydration of African bush
      in the diarrhea of Zanzibar
      in a vial of Pedialyte.
She died the death of a sanctioned Iraqi girl
      no boundaries in sand dug outs
      no penicillin on Acacia trees
      no united way for a sickled tarnished penny.
She has joined the blood river of twisted carcass.

My eyelids are screens to the backdrop of his tumbling tomb.
The fallen man is falling.
Some anonymous cadaver is falling.
He is the rain of descending graves
      prostituted bird droppings
      falling vertical assembly line
      stock falling into a Korean labor of child heap
      falling into the noise of *majnun*
      crowd space crashing skulls of shattered mosaics
      into the open cave of zero
      falling down into the urban scrotum of Harlem
      into the closed palate of chocolate slavery
      into decapitated Taser breath
      into forgotten blankets of small pox
      you know those forgotten blankets of small pox
      Trail of Tears — Trail of Tears
      heart falling heat fixed into the stain of microbes
      into an anthrax wail of crows
      falling up the vertebrae of post-modernist architecture

Have you seen Mary Maryam Malaika Marta? Ah, Marta

Her hair is rain forests, each strand a disciple of its own.
She is almost *majnun.*
The plague of chemical lake pumps her veins.
Her nipples are a leaky dioxin faucet.
Her baby is a dowry traded to the North Star.
It is a unicorn born deformed in the raw sewage of
Guatemala.
I am almost *majnun.*
      a displaced monsoon/scarf poetry blowing in soot

Have you seen?

The After Death of Birth:
Requiem for a Greenless Forest

To be the long stem after death of birth
Perennial justice of roots rising
Merciful heroine of seeded kernels
Propagator of unhatched blooms

To be the terminal gavel of passion of nature
Is to suffer passion nature
Is to suffer the perfection of grieving foliage
Is to suffer constipated mulch of styrofoam polymers
Is to suffer echo
Hear the
Eulogy of rainforest choirs
Fern homilies
Rupturing throats of declining lilies
Sorrow sighs of sagebrush

Hear the splitting girth of cactus seep
acidic rain onto dying species
Hear trees sizzle shadows from the poach
of extinguishing foresters
Hear the Earth malignantly distort
into inoperative oxygen

I tell you theirs is no ordinary passion—
Green quest of survival
famously impaled as chlorophyll crucifix
rose petaled into industry exploitations

Verdant blood
Theirs is no ordinary passion
To perish seasonally then resurrect in
an ocean valley of extinction
To loiter beneath the solar stream of a
depreciating planet
To expire in the threshold of reincarnations
To usher the descent
To rally the return
To hail the sapling rebirth of water

———————————————

*The poem, "The After Birth of Death," was inspired after looking
into Passion, an acrylic painting rendered by Dr. James Brown.*

Beginning at the End of the Beginning

"It is the end of clocks!"
the announcer yelled,
shouting tall trees down.

Much of flailing humanity was
rushing about
fright-frothing
fear-folding
convulsing into a heap this side of
Earth's exit door.

Terrified believers
like parboiled barn animals were
galloping straight into their flaming dread
lunging through hooplas of white fire –
hypnotized by the seductive orange of red war.

The poem, "Beginning at the End of the Beginning," was inspired after looking into Divine, an acrylic painting rendered by Dr. James Brown.

"Yellow Lives on a Banana!"

(For Robyn)

Fate cracked a smile
and you born from a wish and a clump of blood
chasing the lint in a sunbeam
you are much funnier than that puppy
I had at 10
Protesting binary constructs
you count 1, 3, 4, 5 6 …
Early one a.m. while surveying
the fruit on the kitchen table
you exclaimed,
"Mommy, yellow lives on a banana!"

It was more surreal when you seemed to
prophecy the future
by reading the cracks in the sidewalk
tracing the raised cement with the tap of your toe
with all the conviction of a Broadway character actress
you warned us mortals
"This is not good, there's going to be trouble."

With precision you placed your hands on
that area called the waist to have them slide
down past the part where your hips have yet to grow
Undaunted you repositioned your little fingers
under your armpits
and appeared to strike a pose that
resembled Chicken Little wearing a pink bow

"The Sky God is not happy
no, she's not happy
she's sad."
You were aiming your index
past an atmosphere of invisible rainbows
My eyelids lifted to witness dancing clouds
against the backdrop of a storm

People of the Rain

People of the rain have eyes
that bulge and swim salamanders in optic fluid

They do not roll freely but
stick like wheels of old skates

Sockets ache for lids to rest
concaved un-stretched

Eyes squeak beyond the
swell of humidity

Eyes like dead fish protrude and stare

What of retinas with teeth marks?

People of the rain possess eyes that possess
a sharpened sclera axed the
head of the swimming salamander
ignited pupils carried it for months

What of the digeridoo playing man?
A victim of the rain
What of the thumb-sucking woman?
A victim of the rain
She is a warped violin bow bending
sight in the curve of sorrow
He is blowing time in a marsh of reeds

Lenses pierce damp mist to overcome the mud
thicker than water
they wade the fog looking for the casket
the box of drowned eyes that talk from the grave

Even in the dream of poetry
Eyes paralyze the smell of want
they are wet
they live dangerously saturated with
amphibian eggs in their brains
they are always wet
those people
those Earth oceans of despair

Swirling Agony

The nerve print of turbulence is tilted

I have seen this before in the whiplash of fear.

Sideways I tread the storm.

Boisterously I thrash the waves suffocating in the wind

Upside down drowning in air

Wading blind

Stolen Cocoa Bean Head

This chocolate chip
baked down its legs
got squat in a cookie
said I am the color of caca
I move slower than decomposition
I do not roll
packed in the gulley of middle passage.

This chocolate chip
pressed its arms into a blob
said I have no digital manipulatives
They were chopped off on the selling block
I do not roll
smashed like cargo in sacs of burlap

This chocolate chip
was shoplifted from Liberia
was mass produced in the flavor of chattel
was corrupted by sucrose and
was seduced by Bettye Crocker

This chocolate chip
had its mother homogenized
into a milk factory
for privileged infants
had its language denatured
behind muffled doors of corporate laboratories

had its spirituality poured into molds of
whoring Easter bunnies

This chocolate chip
became the envy of potato chips
became the repugnant desire of vanilla
became a cross-dressing peanut almond and crispy
became the national sweet tooth
became the reason for carob
became the blame of cavities
became the melt of Cesar Chavez
became a laxative
and moved on the backs of migrant workers
from South America to candy-coated minstrel shows

This chocolate chip said
I am that slave ship you wear as a hat
I am the rape of double boilers
I am free-based Hershey bars
I am good company for tar and nicotine
the snort of Swiss miss up your nose
an acne necklace
an acceptable addiction for your children

This chocolate chip said
somewhere in me
there is a cocoa bean
somewhere in me
lives the stolen head of a man

Hey, Big Man

I

Although I wasn't sometimes I think I was there
listening between sirens watching you
an eight-year-old little lord on Mack Ave fat with fear
gracefully dodging bullies at playground time
Like a baby whale harpooned and tied
to your second grade girlfriend
bullyboys dragged you both
alternating kicks
from cancellation shoes they SANG

"HEY BIG MAN: It's raining It's Pouring the Old Man is
Snoring!"

You — the first grandchild lifted high
 then dropped from top of the monkey bars

II

Although you weren't sometimes I think you were here
watching me eat my shredded
adolescence in a bowl of sauerkraut but
you were standing on broken porch steps
reciting the dictionary over a dinner of ketchup soup

When I was small all my insides was an ulcer
at 13 I grew a uterus bled for twenty-three days
Oh what a glorious life to be young and full of menses
trips to the gynecologist office pelvic examines in hiding

I collected alley rocks
rolled them in handkerchiefs
some lace some flowered some to
toss at tall white men who offered me red hots

III

When you were young
you slept on an open mattress and
woke marred by creases and lines
that was a Great Society
a morgue filled with long black carcasses
penises swollen from flame-melted heroin

That was a Great Society with
silver badges and blue bruises
That was a Great Society Horatio Alger and
his boot straps factory
straps securely fastened around your father's neck
a human pendulum swinging from street lamp post
That was a Great Society

with liberals who
shout "IT'S WORST in OTHER PLACES!"
Yeah, like Pluto where it's 900 degrees below zero

IV

This is still a Great Society
This is not Auschwitz
There is a public school system where children line up
Horatio still manufacturing his boot straps
There are babies dying in urban centers
As the bullies jumped up and down on you

they SHOUTED
"Show me your Ketchup smile, Big Man"
The liberals SHOUT
"Don't be a building Big Man
Don't be a man Big Man
Don't be so big Big Man
Remember it's damn cold on Pluto"

Dragon Poem

"One by six… One by six …One by Six… One by six
they Scotch Plaid my walls and paper my closets.
These obnoxious creatures' hearts
in formaldehyde skin breathe no fire.
Romantic reptiles or dinosaur knights
screw-drive my grey matter.
One by six plastic wrapped chameleons
frenzy calm in lunch boxes."

"Just point them out to me and I'll slay everyone," said he.

"They've stolen giraffe wing," I said, "and dart
in ledges of mountain caves.
They've stolen baby doll fins and wade
amidst algae treading the revenge of black moccasins.
They're thieving solace and impersonating ducks.
Woodstock is a dragon that breathes no fire but feathers
silence.
They are shop cart lurking and castle exploding
down 3 a.m. Avenue, courting quiet
with dragon eye in alphabet soup.

Hero of mine: rescue me from scales on tooth brush tails,
canoes down Eustachian tubes, walks with alligator poison.
Knight with poet's knuckles: save me from
pyramid pointed spines, horned tongues, fantasies
in day mirrors.

Spirit conquistador bearing beacon before Christ: preserve
solitude in my honor, weasel climb this fence of fear."

There are dragon plastered windows and
dragons solid still in ice…
Dragons' melting warm wax and
somebody's been sleeping in my bed dragon…
And all my grit and bowl is gone dragon…
And this little wee wee had none dragon…
And occupational nightmare dragon…
And It's the only way to fly dragon…
Jazz desponding revolt dragons /
 don't know and dedicated to nothing dragons/
from baby to beast transition dragons/
all black men are dragons dragons/
decomposed mice in New England Clam politics dragons

Dear giant lizard killer, archaeologist of Grimm's Tales:

Fold the draw bridge up.
One by six…One by six…One by six
they Loch Ness my carpet with clawed memories
One by six they breathe no fire but
appear by the orchard and the subway.

Save me from toilet addicted dragons/
patrons to philosophical dragons/
don't rock the boat or raft dragons/and
the identity crisis of horse dragons/
there is a Chicago Soup line dragon/
smoked bar-be-que dragons/ there are
four score and seven years of
pseudo democratic dragons
that breathe no fire.

And one by six you slay them O' knight with poet's knuckles.

River Killers: Caught!

(This is a performance poem intended for multiple voices.)

Caught   In the under belly of denial
                Killing us is suicidal

Caught   Like a fish in a net
                You'll see our power yet

Caught   Think you have the upper hand
                Uprisings all over this land

Caught   Culture isn't real estate
                Path you pave will be your fate

Caught
Illegitimate
Imposter Poster System
Redemption ain't come yet
You will fall or you will listen
Seeeee

Don't care what the People need
ya don't care
Don't care if the People feed
ya don't care
Don't care if the People bleed

River Killers Horror Show Thrillers
Rivers Killers Agony Deliverers
Daaaaaaaaaammmmmmmm YOU!!!!!!!!!!!!!

Caught   Revisionist history
                   Deceits are blistering

Caught   Pain reign is ending
                   Mutiny is trending

Caught   Stealing water, what?
                   Poisoning water, what?

Caught   Heart pawned for gold
                   You lost your soul

Caught
Wicked Illusionist
Community Contortionists
Lead lynch lead lynch lead lynch policy strings
death Screams death screams death screams death screams
Seeeee

Don't care what the People need
ya don't care
Don't care if the People feed
ya don't care
Don't care if the People bleed and bleed and bleed

River Killers Horror Show Thrillers
Rivers Killers Hate Monument Builders
Daaaaaaaaaaammmmm YOU!!!!!!!!!!!!!!!!

(Little Girl River)
Excuse me, excuse me, Mama Semaj
Excuse me, but I have a question:
If they kill the water, then they kill me,
the tree, the wildebeest, and the bee
I am Little Girl River trying to understand
Why do they bloody the People?
Why they you bloody the People?
Why they you bloody the People and the land?

Caught Caught Caught Caught Caught Caught Caught

Caught   Institutionalized the sky

Caught   Institutionalized your lies

Caught   Institutionalized my Mother

Caught   Institutionalized my Father

Caught   13 deaths and counting
                Brain damage mounting

Caught
You are guilty
of massive cruelty
criminal deeds
homage to greed criminal deeds

Don't care what the People need
ya don't care
Don't care if the People Feed
ya don't care
Don't care if the People bleed

River Killers Horror Show Thrillers
River Killers Diabolic Leaders

Daaaaaaaaammmmmm YOU!!!!!!!!!

(Finale)
Climbing down a mountain in the Glue Trap of Rodents
Climbing down a mountain in the Glue Trap of Rodents
Climbing down a mountain in the Glue Trap of Rodents
Climbing down a mountain in the Glue Trap of Rodents

(Repeat)

Caught in the rain
Caught in the rain
Caught driving pain
Caught driving pain
Caught covering shame
Caught hiding blame
Caught hiding blame

Caught playing sane
Caught playing sane

Ca-ught   Ca-ught   Ca-ught   Ca-ught!

When Fools Talk to Me

Considering the present climate, I find myself adjusting spectacles a great deal as I encounter the latest absurdity du jour in a wave of micro-aggressions. The idea of the word *micro-aggression* is actually a double upside down insult, as there is nothing, nothing minor or micro about these aggressive assaults! One never knows when or why the next eyeglasses adjustment will be necessary. Lunacy seems to be mounting by the minute.

When fools talk to me, adjusting my glasses affords me the extra two seconds necessary to assess, think, compartmentalize, remain silent or speak clearly, or be kind and compassionate, or breathe and breathe again, or run the entire U.S. history through my mind, flip cards bending and falling, falling, or offer tutorials in systemic oppression — on systemic everything, or make a date to do lunch in between broadcast murders of unarmed Black men, or laugh madly at the absurdity just uttered to my face, or cry fire through my eyes, or consider becoming a recluse, or stab a poem in its heart, or jump wildly in thick air, push off on the diving board of ignorance into another dimension.

When fools talk to me, those two seconds of eyeglasses adjustment give me the stillness required to pray, call on ancestors, talk to them about sister Sandra Bland, remember my training, light candles, expose illusions of power, make an incision:

a topographical deconstructionist cross- section slit around the throat of fake democracy — you know, do a lobotomy on false scripture; carbon date the madness, know the lie, pardon the brainwashed messenger baring toxins for they know not what they say or do, disengage, rally the angels, take cover, kaboom false evidence appearing real because they know exactly what they do, liquefy in ultraviolet brilliance, transform into the Sun, a glowing cauldron winged woman floating on an electric carpet above it all!

When fools talk to me, those two seconds are perspective in formation, certainty lining up on Mercury. Saturn satellites transmit Gamma Ray energy to my private electromagnetic field as I sit in the neon sky on an infrared chariot in my corner office. I walk down the street, pass a cave of buried choke-holding policies, and I sling shoot boomerang, shoot boomerang, shoot boomerang one million micro-aggressions from my orbit, repelled like projectile vomiting over the indigenous rainbow like a sports foul out of bounds that snags on edges of jagged clouds. And Ray Charles sings: "Hit the road, and don't cha come back no more no more no more no more; hit the road, and don't cha, don't cha, don't cha, don't cha….

The axis of our planet straightens. Untruths that pollute bow, bow, bow down and disintegrate into the debris of a sneeze. Ahchew! The atmosphere is activated. The moon, my ride and die, pulls water strings uuupppp, the sea high-fives in wave gesture as hate evaporates. Gravity genuflects. There is a hierarchical reset.

There is a hierarchical reset. There is a hierarchical reset. Nature is taking over. Me and swag dance around the shrinking fool, the fool sitting across from me, shrinking like reverse osmosis, shrinking like a wart in a TV advertisement. He is one foot tall now, the insulting non-relevant, inconsequential fool, fool of supposed unintended assaults. The micro-aggression maker to all things decent and good is the size of a dog biscuit—one-half inch, two millimeters.

I lower my eyeglasses and peer at this tiny, corrupted, ill-guided soul, who once wore the smirk of privilege. I watch it rewind its birth until it disappears—vanishes — gone! All I need, all I need: two seconds, two seconds to adjust these spectacles. You see, when fools talk to me, *moi*, magical things — like cosmic power things — happen; but I need at least two seconds, two seconds and some very large eyeglasses.

"The divine impulse, it's always safe to follow it. We've got to trust it and go wherever it takes us. Especially women."

Ruby Dee

Infernos and Inspiration

Investigating Infernos and Inspirations

Welcome to the season of fire! The poems in this section glow a sky-tall blue; they are of the flaming, ferocious, blazing installations that melt the air and combust dreams. These poems and the introductory prose cannot be contained, as they fire ball leap through history into film and theater and production, and into the hearts of the incinerated. These words so candled — are poems that engulf. They are painfully personal, yet freeing.

Surfing the Wave Rock

The poem, "Wave Rock," spawned without moisture in an arid sack. In my living room, I lay in stupor upon a field of sunburned carpet, legs like petrified branches crossed in a crime scene, my arm a tolerant log for my head to rest, breathing so shallow I could be pronounced dead. I wasn't. But, I wasn't living either. I was suspended in canicular mourning, levitating grief in the state of in-between.

> **"You Can't Clock the Rock, You Can't Stop the Wave"** That's for you Mommy, that's Wave Rock, **You Can't Clock the Rock, You Can't Stop the Wave,** that's for you mommy, that's Wave Rock!"

From my disintegrating tomb, my upper appendages limped and shuffled on parched hands to push my dehydrated torso perpendicular to the floor. Sitting as broken kindle wood, I was a rocking chair crumbling to sawdust. I faced a wall of glaring windows. The open sky wore a foreboding brightness that almost pushed me back to my ground level cave. My eyelids, glued and dried by gravity, bore the weight of an abandoned rusty draw bridge that could not hoist despite attempts. Retracted cheek muscles squeezed crow's feet into accordion pleats to leverage the lift. Squinting, barely prying open planks of hardened eye tissue to a sliver, I could almost see my legal pad and pen only a stretch away.

Emotional rigor mortis had set in, as every filament, every vein and artery was stiff with misery. I inched toward the lined yellow paper to scribble dictates from ether, from Robyn, my newly departed daughter, who was instructing me via spiritual satellite to breathe in the message of *Wave Rock*. I was to write it, study it, and follow it, all while self-incinerating— all while I was bleeding fire.

"You Can't Clock the Rock You Can't Stop the Wave.
That's for you, Mommy. That's the *Wave Rock*."

The lines of this couplet pooled like droplets swelling into a rising sea, tides rolling into a tsunami for justice. *Wave Rock* was more than an anthem for oppressed people, which alone would have been a gift. It was more than a womanist manifesto; that too would have been a treasure. I have always been a poet for suffocated voices. *Wave Rock* was forced nature, consuming me, to save me from the inferno that was extinguishing me by the minute by the day.

Once my mind received my daughter's voice echoing what would become the essential chorus of *Wave Rock,* I was on a fulfillment mission: *Wave Rock,* the poem, morphed into *Wave Rock,* the musical soundtrack. First, I counseled with Brother Dawud: "What was the meaning behind this gift of extended metaphor?" He answered with the badest bass riff ever, which became the introductory and driving pulse of the musical soundscape.

At that time, my poetic domain was largely odd meters and polyrhythms, more like Charlie Parker or Faruq Z. Bey than the repetitiveness of a disco beat. But did *Wave Rock* require something different from my comfortable Out-Cat, freestyle structure? I declared, "I will go 4/4!" Undaunted, I wrestled content into form, creating a consistent wave that people could ride.

I visited Bert's Place for the express purpose of finding JB (Dr. James Brown) to assist me with perfecting 4/4 rhythms. He was a drummer noted for holding down the bottom in his music ensemble, the Millennium Drummers. The rehearsal date was set. Echoes of my mother's etiquette so engrained in me raised the question: What will you serve this wayfarer who travels to assist you? I was quite the cook — or I had been. Following my daughter's death, everything I stirred on that stove, I burned, and if my intention was to roast or sauté, I blackened. I decided bag salad would be safe. While in the market, I hazarded to purchase a pound of ground turkey.

Turkey burger and salad was a hit. JB was notably appreciative, "Semaj," he said, drawing out my name into three syllables with a big smile, "You're feeding me like I've never been fed before!" I smiled demurely. Turning to look from my ninth floor window, I was surprised to see signs of spring, buds on trees and the state bird, a robin. In our four-hour session, we recorded the beats that set the tempo and underlining rhythm for what was growing into a grand production.

In the final recording, JB's djembe galloped, made war, kept pace, and just jammed.

Having lived my life in the realm of the acoustic, I continued my search for a new sound – something different, for which I did not have a name. I visited technological genius, Baba Heru, who was creating strangely beautiful electronic music. It was cutting edge. I did not understand the processes. I listened to several pieces and was intrigued. I purchased the preeminent sound of *Wave Rock*. It was ethereal, a foreboding, moving musical mystery.

Meanwhile, I received a call from Brooklyn. Jasmine Murrell, an internationally renowned artist, then a recent Parson's School of Design graduate, was deft at trying to convince me that I had agreed in the previous year to be the subject of an art video. "No, Jasmine, I remember no such thing." Jasmine was coming to Detroit in less than a month to capture the *Wave Rock*. Arranging and rearranging the score consumed me.

But, who would sing the chorus that swam continuously in my mind? Mama Het, who was the second half of the stalwart marriage of Heru and Het, cut searing lead chorus vocals. Her voice was beautiful, haunting. My dear friend, Arlene Williams brought a unique, other world quality to the chorus, lifting it to yet another level.

A journalist who came to cover the *Wave Rock* phenomenon for a major newspaper could not deny the energy, broke protocol and dove into the wave, lending striking soprano dexterity under a pseudonym.

Wave Rock, true to its chorus, will not be stopped. It is a powerful poem that asserts the will of the people. It became a lyrical soundscape to an iconic art/social justice video by Jasmine Murrell. *Wave Rock* is a spontaneous art collective, a production performed by various musicians and vocalists at Michigan Opera House, Mt. Elliot Park, Millennium Theater, the Charles H. Wright Museum of African American History, and elsewhere. Its creative energy helped to fuel the marriage between Semaj and James Brown, MD. It is a literary study; it affects and engulfs people from Detroit to New York to Cali and London. *Wave Rock* was instrumental in restoration of my life, infusing me with the indelible spirit of the wave and the time-honored body as rock. Long live the *Wave Rock!*

Wave Rock

(Inspired by Robyn Sampson, September 29, 1993 – July 14, 2000)

You Can't Clock the Rock
You Can't Stop the Wave
You can't clock the rock
You can't stop the wave

 I rock waves
        from the tears of screaming fish heads
                                rock slaves
from the jailed reflection of Mumia
                                rock graves
        halitosis of invisible assassins
        from the space-less places colors float
        from the clam-shelled tomb of poverty

        You can't clock this
        You can't stop this
        Can't clock the rock
Can't stop the Wave Rock

You can't clock this
You can't stop this
Can't clock the rock
Can't stop the Wave Rock

You can't clock the rock
You can't stop the wave
You can't clock the rock
You can't stop the wave

I rock to appropriate myself
                          I rock to exonerate
                 the stale sardines of canned ocean

          Invert the mirror of un-netted mackerels
                          Bail from the kelp beds of
asphyxiation

away from the coral morgue of
indigenous annihilation
I rock to appropriate
                          I rock to exonerate

          I rock to recreate myself
to free to free to free to free to free to free to free to free
                          Something
          You can't clock this
          You can't stop this
          Can't clock the rock
Can't stop the Wave Rock

          You can't clock this
          You can't stop this
          Can't clock the rock
Can't stop the Wave Rock

You can't clock the rock
You can't stop the wave
You can't clock the rock
You can't stop the wave

I do a deoxygenated rock
into the current of sunlight
onto the hot coals of belligerent oysters
        beyond the brand of sacred snails
I rock-a- burn burrn
Rock-a-burn burrrnn
Rock-a-burn burrrrrrn
into my authentic
into my authentic
        into my authentic Self

till beams eat me like cannibal eels
                till I'm seduced by an electric fin
        till I become amphibian amphibian amphibian
Fire   Water Wind
        till oil bursts into flaming calabash of Quran

7 layers of veils extinguished from my face
My skeleton a fried fetus
My lover a horizontal dessert awaits

        You can't clock this
        You can't stop this
        Can't clock the rock
Can't stop the Wave Rock

        You can't clock this and
        You can't stop this
        Can't clock the rock
Can't stop the Wave Rock

You can't clock the rock
You can't stop the wave
You can't clock the rock
You can't stop the wave

And I
rock to the pour of prisoned sand
to the poisoned pulse of an occupied land
and I
rock in the growth of gill tumors
and I
rock with perpetual fools
and I
rock to up rock the intensity in urban density
I rock to up rock the intensity in urban density
I rock to up rock the intensity in urban density

I rock to up rock the intensity in urban density
     And I rock slow
like like stop action photography
     And I rock slow
like like justice wading
     And I rock slow like like like like

I rock fast like
gurgling insomniac panting

        piranha drum crashing
        liquid apocalypse smashing
        aboriginal schizophrenics laughing

I do the rock of ages
rock tides rock cries
Diallo lies
           in deprivation devastation ebb
It rocks my head the webs we bed

And I flow
           while dying in the sneeze of obscurity
           while drinking salt sapphire of inferiority
           while bowing to the sea mountain
           of my elegantly shrouded daughters
           my elegantly shrouded daughters
     You can't clock this
     You can't stop this
     Can't clock the rock
Can't stop the Wave Rock

     You can't clock this
     You can't stop this
     Can't clock the rock
Can't stop the Wave Rock

You can't clocka the rocka
You can'ta stopa the wave
You can'ta clocka the rocka
You can'ta astopa the wave

In the plastic spirit of plastic
In the plastic spirit of plastic

On the wave of precipice
like lynched lobsters hanging hanging

loose as fish scaled dangling dangling

As bought meat we boil
in the war on domestic soil

I rock waves
Trail of Tears Ocean Skulls 400 years
I rock waves
sweat shop houses dye-stained blood for pretty blouses
I rock waves
migrant workers multinationals toxic servers
I rock waves
misogyny violence till it's quelled I won't be silenced
I rock waves
homeless madness zero cradle spiritual sadness
I rock waves
pendulum breeze wind tocks truth of infinity
                              truth of infinity

Earthquake the sleeping
        Children are dying our planet is weeping
Earthquake the sleeping
        Children are dying our planet is weeping
Earthquake the sleeping
        Children are dying our planet is weeping
Earthquake the sleeping
        Children are dying our planet is weeping

Earthquake the sleeping
> Children are dying our planet is weeping (Repeat)
> Children are dying our planet is weeping (Repeat)

Rock free
Rock free
Rock Yemaya
Rock Mami Wata
Rock free
Rock fantasies
Rock frenzy
Rock frantic

I do the rainbow rock
I do the rain-soul rock
I do the rain-cold rock
> I do a plain ole-rock
And I rock   ON!
Repeat:
Chorus, refrain and improvisation

> You ought to be free you got to rock free
> You got to got to rock free

Account of Tongue, Tongued: Poem Captivity

It's June in Detroit. I am at the J. Rainey Art Gallery, viewing a three-inch thick, 4 x 6 feet slab of golden honey-colored pinewood that has been shellacked to a glass-like sheen. It hangs prominently on the wall. The pine knots are rich, dark dimensional swirls, that I imagined as eyes staring up at me when as a girl playing on Aunt Jackie's living room knotty pine floor. Uncle Thomas, her husband prided himself in maintaining that triple gloss of polyurethane. I would pretend it was an ice skating rink and slide across, socks as blades. Busy reminiscing, I did not wonder why a beautiful, flattened piece of wood was on display in the loft balcony under the signage of the artist, Jasmine Murrell.

Despite its being lodged in the rear of an abandoned furniture factory, surrounded by bumpy weeds and debris, the gallery aesthetic was in sync with my sensibilities — urban chic, sleek, finished — none of that post-industrial rustic romanticizing. I imagined myself weightless, in a more cosmopolitan place, a city not beleaguered by decades of institutional discrimination, red lining, covenants, an under-resourced school system, and the massive decline of the automobile industry. I leaned into a feeling of being nowhere. My daughter was with Grandma having proper tea, dissecting Duke Ellington, making banana rice bread. Everything was *irie* — peaceful.

I returned my smile to the shiny wood in front of me. I always loved trees. I gazed into the glistening grain, and in slow motion, the patterns in the wood gradually penetrated my mind, staining my brain with staggering imagery: On the knotty swirl of pine, there was a faint line, a squiggle of red that dropped low and swung limp, like a body dangling from a bloated black head, which only seconds ago was just a mere rounding of knotty pine. My wider lens revealed the images repeating, punctuating the wooden canvas, exposing a vast expanse of murder, a wide cross-section of almost invisible lynchings. No longer in the pristine gallery, I was transported to the defiled woods of Mississippi, 1920. My eyeballs began a rapid shift from limb to branch, and in a desperate attempt to shelter from the horror, from the sight of Miss Martha and Big Red burnt and castrated and little baby twins suspended in death fire, I thrust my hand into my head, ripping my eyes from their sockets, shoving them into my purse. I ran blindly down the stairs, and catapulted to my car, where I tried to outdrive Terror, but Terror was just outside the window, keeping up with my little GMC Tracker. I thought to out run it, taking the elevator, but Terror took the stairs and met me at my apartment door. I pushed past, knocking it aside, but Terror bulldozed in and threw me to the floor, pounding my chest like a giant white gorilla. I scuffled and wailed and convulsed until the poem, "Tongue, Tongued," was written. I was exhausted and used. I have since named this painful creative process, *poem captivity*.

The poem, "Tongue, Tongued," introduced me to the historical figure, Anastacia, a beautiful young enslaved African woman who was subjected to the cruelty of being made to wear an iron face mask. Anastacia is now a Catholic saint venerated in Brazil. This experience of *poem captivity* compelled me to reflect on the wisdom of a line from Gwendolyn Brooks's poem, "To the Diaspora:" "Africa is in me...."

"Tongue, Tongued" is a poem about a time when a female figure emerges from the *Tongue, Tongued Nation* with the super powers of revelation, retribution and retaliation. In this time, all of the heinous acts committed against women throughout the ages are experienced by the perpetrators:

> "You will begin to eat the tea cup you sip and
> You will strangle on your imploded tongue of
> lynched spaghetti and
> You will gargle on the indigestible teeth of
> slavery and
> You will be raped by your own gallery
> Coiling itself into the memory of snake
> messengers
> Circulating your throat becoming a brace of
> reptilian restraints…"

The benefits of years have afforded me a twenty-first century interpretation of this work. I truly believe that the *ONE* referred to in the poem symbolizes *each one*, every woman rising against systemic oppression, loving and teaching one another about their worth. I further know the *ONE* includes men who vie for justice for women. *ONE* is the bleeding fire of unity, the ability to transcend by tapping into the eternal spring of regenerative light.

About the Artist

Jasmine Murrell is a Detroit-born, Brooklyn–based international visual artist. She is a graduate of Parsons School of Design and Hunter College.

Jasmine Murrell: "I make work about miracles, miracles that happen in the worst of times and in the most invisible places. I use a wide rage of media including installation, sculpture, land art, and film to invoke a transformative experience around historical erasures."

Notes on "Tongue, Tongued"

"Tongue Tongued: Tongue Tongued" became the title cut of a poetry album that I released in 2000, with the late great Faruq Z. Bey as Musical Director. "Tongue, Tongued" became a poetry production premiering at the Millennium Theater in Southfield, Michigan (2002), with special guests, The Last Poets. Kimberli Boyd was the choreographer. I was joined by a host of dancers and musicians: The late Faruq Z. Bey as musical director, Ras Kente, Sunkaru Clifford Sykes, Issa Abralameem, Wayne Wardlow, Riva Stewart, Fonz, and Michelle Jahra McKinney. The Little Sister Robyn Youth Poetry Contest winners were announced. Media coverage included five newsprint articles, a performance on public television's "Back Stage Pass," and two interviews on WDET public radio. It was a large production. Folks flew in from the Big Apple. Compliments of culinary taste master, Arlene Williams, there was delectable spread of gourmet food available for all the artists backstage. As we used to say: *It was all the Way Live!*

Tongue, Tongued

Among the people of the Tongue Tongued
Among the people of the Pierced Tongue
Among the people of the Tongue Pierced

It is said… It is said…It is said!
That there would come One…One …One!
That there would come One!

Who would burn through bars
One!
Who would sear time onto a canvas of skin
One!
Who would send horror into a mixture of acrylic and blood
One!
Who would erupt from a combusting Jasmine seed!

Among the people of the Tongue Tongued
Among the people of the Pierced Tongue
Among the people of the Tongue Pierced

It is said… It is said…It is said!
That there would come one!
That the brand of shredded vulvas
vomits into a floating cloud of decay and
It is said!
that many upon seeing her will stampede their own charred
core
to flee the wind of truth and

It is said!
It will rain puddles of their putrid flesh
that of menses and dried syrup
The stench of plasticized chocolate
dangling on the hinge of a crocodile bite
And it is said!
It is said! It is said!
One glance at her framed salt and
you will fade into the spiritual sculpture of eye into
the hypnotized images of contorted cacao breast and
you will begin to eat the tea cup you sip and
you will strangle on your imploded tongue of lynched
spaghetti and
you will gargle on the indigestible teeth of slavery and
you will be raped by your own gallery
coiling itself into the memory of snake messengers
encircling your throat becoming a brace of reptilian restraints

And it is said!
upon seeing her
you will contract to the knees of Brazil
your face reflecting in the steel muzzle of Anastasia
And it is said
it is said
upon witnessing her
you will constrict to the defiant quicksand of Madagascar
to the caged Hottentot One
to your pivot trying to escape the vile consumption of
freedom

Among the people of the Tongue Tongued
Among the people of the Pierced Tongue
Among the people of the Tongue Pierced

It is said… It is said…It is said!
That there would come One…One …One!
That there would come One!
One!

Meeting Mother Ocean

(Making of the New Tribe)

I had not written a poem in over a decade. I was busy creating "Onion Revolt," a one-woman comedy on the nutritional value of vegetables, where I played 14 different characters to the magical musical accompaniment of my husband, Dr. James Brown. Before that project, I was writing copy for the "Dr. James Brown Radio Broadcast," and then writing a story cookbook, *Feasts and Fables from the Planted Kingdom with Lyrical CD.* As Director of Community Outreach for James Brown, MD PLC, I wrote and facilitated health education workshops throughout Genesee County, Michigan, servicing the American Heart Association, Genesee County Medical Alliance, churches, community centers, and schools. The poison water crisis in Flint compelled me to initiate an art curriculum with the Flint chapter of *Pierians, Incorporated.* I also wrote a science curriculum, *7 Biology Experiments: Explorations in the Scientific Method*, and facilitated a workshop along with my husband for the Detroit Independent Freedom Schools at the Charles H. Wright Museum of African American History in Detroit. Yes, I had been busy, busy writing, but not poetry.

This changed with Mr. Jerry Taliaferro's photographic exhibit at the Flint Institute of Arts (FIA). Nominated by Mrs. Velynda Makhene, I accepted the honor of being a portrait subject in the *Women of a New Tribe* exhibit. The photo session stirred something in me. Quietly I uttered, "I feel like I could write something about this." Mr. Taliaferro and Ms. Sarah Kohn, FIA assistant curator, responded with a polite nod.

Exiting the FIA premises, feeling richly inspired, I returned to my world of many projects and deadlines, and thought nothing further of "Women of a New Tribe."

After the gallery's reveal, nine months later, Velynda and her husband, Dr. Ramotsumi Makhene, hosted a fabulous afterglow at their home for FIA luminaries, friends, and the honored guest, artist/photographer, Mr. Jerry Taliaferro. The astounding life-sized black and white photographs of Flint women had cast a mesmerizing effect over the evening. Velynda asked me to read comments that she thought I had written about the exhibit "I didn't write anything," I regretfully explained to her. Velynda insisted I did. "You wrote something, you probably forgot." "Velynda, I would remember that." This comedic to and fro banter resolved with me offering to write and read something for the afterglow that would be held 72 later! "I will write a brief appreciation note," so I thought.

Once I began to sketch and outline, it became apparent that this was not a note, but a big poem coming through. Oh, my writing process is strange. I could feel a faraway rumble, a roar, like a locomotive or ocean. I called my sister, Lynn, who listened and commented. Those preliminary notes moved me closer to the core of the writing. I called Cousin Linda, and with controlled apprehension, confided that a big poem was coming: "I am going to write a poem!" Linda, always poised and serene in demeanor, seemed to steady herself as she inquired, "What type of poem, Semaj?" I responded, "I'm not sure. I see an ocean, a sky, waterfalls, and skulls at the bottom. It's about us, our story. It's our story. There is sorrow and ebullient joy! The name of the exhibit is *Women of a New Tribe*. The question begs, what happened to the old tribe and how did the new tribe become new?

This poem will be named "The Making of a New Tribe (Mother Ocean)." That night, praying as I fell asleep, I asked that an

126

extraordinary work would come forth for the women, and for all people, and that it would be a painless creative process, that I would not be affected adversely by it. I did not want to be emotionally stuck at the bottom of the Atlantic Ocean! My wish was granted. At dawn, I felt like a scribe, taking notes from inside myself. When I read what I had written, I barely understood the layered meanings.

This time Cousin Linda called me. After I recited the poem, the air was moist with tears. Those speechless moments gave me pause. I was shocked. Why was Linda crying? "Semaj, your authentic voice has returned. This is vintage Semaj; it aligns with your previous work," Linda said with quiet intensity. I could tell she really wanted me to understand the gravity of what was happening. I was happy twice over, as she was clearly moved, and I had the rare benefit of being spared the emotional turmoil and weight of the poem!

Zipppitydoda! I had surmised poetry departed long ago with my beloved daughter, Robyn, never to return. I was just grateful I was not rolling in grief after having written a poem about immeasurable loss. Wisdom spoke from inside of me: "Like the women of a new tribe, you're on the other side of all of that. The time of rolling in grief is over." I read the poem to my dear sister-friend, Dr. Gloria House, (Aneb

Kgositsile), noted poet, professor emeritus and human rights icon. She cautioned me not to be surprised by the response I would receive from the audience. Dr. House characterized the poem as a gift. Then, once I read it to my husband, everything started to happen.

My handsome hero is motion maker. Enthused, he offered to accompany me with his Arborlune™, an instrument he invented from a backyard tree branch. This instrument has beautiful tones, like bass and bassoon calling from another world. That night we performed at the Makhenes' home. The enthusiasm was enormous. Mr. John B. Henry, Executive Director of the Flint Institute of Arts asked us to present this work the next day at the 10th Annual Community Gala, where Mr. Jerry Taliaferro's work would be honored. Dr. House was correct: the poem had touched, moved, clarified, unearthed and held up my African American sisters in a unique manner that all women and men could celebrate. Although I had been warned, I wasn't ready for the tears, confessions, and need to talk and touch me, the author. Then memory rushed me like a wave. This is the way it had been 14 years earlier before I stopped writing poetry. Still, I wondered what I was in for, questioning if I wanted to be the messenger whose writing affected people on such a deep level — and then worried whether I had any choice in the matter.

Changes, and more changes. The poem grew. It generated another invitation to perform for the FIA event, *Meet the Women of a New Tribe*, and it elicited an invitation from Dr. House to perform the poem at the Charles H. Wright Museum of African American History to benefit the Detroit Freedom Schools Movement and the Museum. The poem grew into a chapbook, complete with an appendix of educational references, a wonderful tool for teaching poetry, history, literary art, and social justice, concurrently or separately. It grew a foreword by esteemed writer Ms. Aurora Harris, and back cover notes by Ms. Marissa Pierce. It grew into a recording at the Boys and Girls Club of Greater Flint (Chief Executive Officer, Mr. Tauzzari Robinson, Director of Programming and Operations, Ms. Amber Miller), with engineer Pharlon Randall working technical, creative magic.

It grew into a debut for Dr. James Brown's invention, the Arborlune ™. Finally, Dr. Brown offered the assessment: "This is no longer a poem; it's theater."

The cover illustration by Ms. Amanda Thomason made me weep. For the first time, I was confronted with the gravity of the words I had written. Her art blasted through my anesthetized bubble with its explicitly frightening skulls and other images – so much so that I strongly considered not using it. My husband vied for it. We took an informal survey, and discovered that the graphics that initially repelled me, others vigorously embraced. Accepting Amanda's cover was a moment of growth for me.

I grew also from a gift of wisdom from nonagenarian Mrs. Edith Prunty Spencer, Flint's first African American librarian. Her words offered me clear direction. After my performance of "Mother Ocean" at the FIA, she asked, "You do a lot of things, don't you?"

"Yes ma'am," I responded.

"Stick with the words, stick with the words. Do you understand?"

"Yes, I now understand, and I will do so. Thank you, Mrs. Spencer."

Mother Ocean
(Making of a New Tribe)

I talked to the Ocean.
I asked Mother Ocean,
How long, how long after Middle Passage
did it take to heal your daughters, make them
whole?

How did you shape this distinct, beautiful
creation?
Mother Ocean answered with serenity:

"It's been 400 years.
I sculpted them from promise.
They were complete in the beginning, throughout,
and remain whole today.
Their memory was stolen. Their memory was
stolen.
Could not remember gold of Benin
or family compounds
Alkebulan antiquity birthing science
Moorish Spain
Timbuktu world center of trade and scholarship
or origins of iron forged French Quarter
Could not remember the military brilliance of
Queen Nzinga
or their original tongues of Fula and Yoruba."

**The waves began to swell and break,
Mother Ocean continued:**

"I fashioned each death new,
molded feminine fluid into flesh
pooling ancient memories floating in time.
They were re-created from the scaring flow of
centuries,
formed by amniotic river that pulses their veins.
They speak the language of water now.
Water is spirit, and spirit remembers.
I am Ocean, remembering when they cannot.

Water is spirit, and spirit remembers.
I am the Ocean spirit remembering, when they
cannot.

My daughters came to me, Mother Ocean,
as cargo in chains on death vessels that heaved
frothy
blood in the crest of my waves.

My daughters came to me, Mother Ocean,
shredding skin, decomposing wombs,
fodder for sea monsters and
New World rapists.

Millions, and millions, and millions, and millions,
and
millions, and millions, and millions, millions

collapsed into the inconceivable lap of violating
current
descended to maritime grave
asphyxiated on the horror of what was yet to be
suffered.

On my ocean floor,
I rocked them in a crucible of seaweed and succor
coddled them in the ebb of coral incantations
washed them with those two aquatic lovers
hydrogen and oxygen.
I cleaned and christened,
purified, baptized their white bone skeletons
in briny blessed assurance.

And as Ocean, as Ocean I followed
that tide of dripping gore across myself
to the shore of servitude.

I never left my daughters; I persisted in all my
forms
sometimes water vapor whispering dignity
sometimes hail storm summoning
strength from Ella Baker Ancestors!"

Again, I asked, Mother Ocean:
How long, how long after Jim Crow did it
take
to make your daughters whole?
Mother Ocean lifted,

waves rose and fell like flying blue tarpaulin,
floods surged dredging sand and
civilization into her amorphous body. She
spoke:

"Seems like eternity, yet it is a drop.
But in every drop there exists eternity.
They were always whole
even with captured memory
even with lynching
Tulsa Holocaust
execution of their God-Men husbands
mass incarceration
medical apartheid
water-boarded psyche
they were always whole.

My daughter's brains are incredible
masterful
cerebral filtering systems
always filtering
filtering faith from fear
hope from horror
triumph from trauma
Get Ye Behind Me
No weapons formed against me
I'm not giving that any energy

Filters
An anointed Amazing Grace Sieve
where Grey Matter that matters lives
These daughters of Ocean
of rain and drizzle
of water cycle alchemy
of aqua rising from the entrails of Atlantic
ascend with the power of bubbling geyser
shooting aspirations vertical from the deep silt of
sea,
made fertile with blood from their people.
They are Reverse Waterfalls Standing Erect!
standing on testament of swirling ancestors
reverse waterfalls standing erect—Standing on
Water!

Standing in boardrooms — Say her name
Standing in courtrooms — Say her name
Standing in legislatures — Say her name
Standing in hospitals- Say her name
Standing on corners — Yes, say her name
Standing in shelters — Yes, say her name
Standing in uniform — Say her name
Standing in science —Say Her Name
Standing in educational institutions - Say her
name

Standing as artists, as athletes, entrepreneurs
at counters, in kitchens, with blue collars and
white collars
in service, as waitresses, and secretaries
Standing in wealth and affluence and
Standing in poverty, in poverty standing on her
knees,
Standing on her knees in poverty, standing on her
knees
on her knees in prayer, in churches
on her knees, in prayer in mosques,
on her knees, in synagogues, praying on her knees
at

altars of indigenous ritual ...
Staaaannnnding with Humaaaaannnnity
Standing up, up Standing up, up Standing up, up
Grandmothers and grandchildren
Standing up, up

Standing, Standing, Standing as unlikely activists
in Lansing capital against state sponsored
poisoning of 100,000 Flint residents!
Mother of Eden
original proto-type of opaque skin,
with eyes of stained glass wisdom and
legacy washed hair, gravity defying hair,
antenna to rainforest galaxy
hair stretching toward Sirius B Star heaven hair
of quantum wave, celestial strands

Water is spirit and spirit remembers.
Water is spirit and spirit remembers.
Call it
Call it
Call it our Ocean intuition
Call it
Call it grit
Call it Holy Ghost
Call it ancestral angel fire
Call it Black Girl Magic!
How else can you explain these
hidden figures, female frequencies sculpting
formation with water pick chisel?

How else can you explain
an Oprah, Nina Simone, Mrs. Edith Spencer,
Dr. Jemison, Dr. Gloria House, Ava DuVernay,
General Harriet Tubman, Mother James,
Michelle Obama, and fifty, fifty, fantabulous Flint
women
of distinction who represent named and unnamed
showering constellations of super nova stars
who became, who are the
"Women of a New Tribe!?"

The Birthing of Womb Is

(Remembering Laurie)

She was iron lace, delicate steel, chiseled features. She sang with the precision of a songbird whistle. Laurie asked me to write something for the sisters, for the women with "eeerrr" flexing petite muscles under flowing chiffon. She wanted to duet with me; include the cut on her album as she was off to record in New York, then Atlanta. Silly, I thought this my opportunity to pen a rap, but I do not write rap, and though I attempted, I wrote Womb IS, a classical blend of jazz, call and response gospel, European styled choral poem. Laurie and I performed Womb IS everywhere: churches, mosques, cathedrals, activity centers, women's groups, museums, libraries, theaters and special occasions. We recorded part one with the iridescent tones of a steel drum supplied by a musician, Arlene, Laurie's mom, my dear friend found playing in the Eastern Market. I think his name was Spice. Part two of Womb IS was recorded with the baaaaad riffs of virtuoso guitarist Ras Kente in his Highland Park home recording studio. Laurie and I were on assignment; a mission to uplift women. We decided as women our work had value, and we as artists must be compensated! So, if Laurie got the gig, she owed me $10. If I got the gig, I owed her $10. As we exchanged, what might have been the same ragged 10 dollar bill over 100 times, we laughed and claimed riches, with the glee of girls; we joshed and played make believe; we were spirit divas, resetting the world order —justice for women, one grand *God is the Womb, Womb Is a Woman* performance at a time. I miss you, my sister Laurie, rest in peace and power.

Womb IS: Part 1

(Voices 1 and 2 perform simultaneously)

(Voice 1)
God is the womb. Womb is a woman.
(Voice 2, Singing)
God is the womb. Womb is a woman.

(Voice 1)
God is the womb.
Womb is a woman.
Female frequency you cannot see
you cannot see
She is invisible sitting in the pain of ashes
lying in the ghetto of testosterone
oppressed by sanctions of men

God is the womb. Womb is a woman.
God is the womb. Womb is a woman.
A camouflaged Mary you cannot see
You cannot see this stolen Madonna
You cannot see her children like rats
over waterfalls spilling into a sea of omission
Blamed for the original sin with that type of legacy
how could she win?

God is the womb. Womb is a woman.
God is the womb. Womb is a woman.

At twilight she is a crying loon
at midnight she is a singing moon
You cannot hear You cannot hear
her prayer that deafens to silence
The tides long for her but recede at dawn from her
when it seems she has no choice
but to swallow her weeping voice

God is the womb. Womb is a woman.
God is the womb. Womb is a woman.
She is the ore you strip-mined like an old prostitute
made captive like hyenas in paint
made crippled in fashions of restraint.
She is a shoreline of aborted embryos
women carved out like empty conk shells
or eaten grapefruit

Tell me, how do you rape Imani?
How do you rape Faith?
How do you steal an attribute of the divine?
God is the womb. Womb is a woman.
God is thee womb. Womb is a woman.

Womb IS: Part 2

(This poem is intended to be performed by 2 voices)

Voice 1 and 2 Staccato:

You can't see   You can't see her

You can't see   You can't see her

Voice 1   **Voice 2**

No mater her laughter is a   You can't see
blessing of grace   You just can't see

She sets the standard of   *(repeat) Staccato)*
the human race

Ancient girl heart of a pearl

MGT GCC

Voice 1 and 2 Staccato:

Female frequency that you can't see

You can't see   You can't see her

You can't see   You can't see her

Voice 2 singing:

First Teacher

Voice 1:

Woman

Voice 2 Singing:

Goddess with blisters

Voice 1:

Woman

Voice 2 Singing:

Warrior Sister

Voice 1:

Woman

Voice 2 Singing:

How could you miss her?

Voice 1:

McSquared to the infinite degree

Voice 1 and 2:

Female frequency that you can't see

You can't see   You can't see her

You can't see   You can't see her

Voice 1:	**Voice 2 Singing:**
She holds the codes to the moon and the Stars	Why Can't You see me?
Sisters make like excavators and mine who you are	Why can't you See Me Now?

To be seen you have to see
yourself and

Your ideas cannot die on a shelf and

It's time for women to awake and stand cause

Voice 1 and 2:

God is the womb and womb is a Woman

God is the womb and womb is a Woman

Voice 2 Singing:

Sisters of fire

Voice 1:

Diamonds

Voice 2 Singing:

Daughters of flame

Voice 1:

Rubies

Voice 2 Singing:

Women of Monsoons

Voice 1:

Sapphire

Voice 2:

Command Hurricanes

Make men call your name!!!

Voice 1:   **Voice 2:**

Hepsheptsu, Khadijah,   You can't see
Nzinga, Fatimah!   You just can't see

Explode the horror of   *(repeat) Staccato)*
misogyny

You can't see this
vanishing queen

Original women that defy being

Voice 1 and 2 staccato:

You can't see   You can't see her

You can't see   You can't see her

Voice 1:   **Voice 2:**

Every man had to come   Why can't
through you   you

God made self so he'd   See me?
have to too

He spun around on an atom   Why can't
of light   you see

He spun through space that   me
was your womb that night   now?

We Wear the veil the scarf
a cover

Scientific Madonna

Millennia Mother

Peace is our nature a comforter sure

But

Voice 1 and 2:

We will war so our children will endure

Voice 1:	**Voice 2:**
We will war so our children will endure	Waaaaaaaaarrrrrrrrr

Voice 1 and 2:

You don't see   You don't see her

God is the Womb and Womb is a Woman

God is the womb and Womb is a Woman

Voice 2:

You don't see   You don't see her

Voice 1 and 2:

Female Frequency that you don't see

You don't see her and you don't see me!!!!

God is the womb and womb is a Woman!

God is the womb and womb is a Woman!

God is the womb and Womb is a Wo-maaaan!!!!!!

" With the groove our only guide, we should all be moved…One nation under a groove, gettin' down just for the funk of it"

George Clinton, Gaary Shider, Walter Morrison

Flames and Flares

Discovering Flames and Flares

It is time to parrrrteee, to dance with the writings in this section. *Flames* honor the warmth of infatuation. *Flares* spark in the realm of spontaneity. Serendipitous are the tones that crescendo, swirl whimsy, twirling an intense musicality, particularly in the poem, "I Left My Dancing Shoes at Home." The tempos and content of these poems are fun, infused with playful sensuality, as in the cosmos space love of "Light Spectrum*.*" The poem, "What If, Then," burns with the delicious intensity of unrequited desire, a desire that traverses continents and centuries. Female sexual power reigns unparalleled in "Black Widow Spider 1 and 2*.*" The black widow spider "…flirts with her prey, then she puts them away!" Mic drop, boom!

What If, Then

What if I am infatuated
with your voicemail the
expectant beep plays
a minor bridge in It Must Have Been Moon Glow

What if you are the Headless Horseman
galloping through centuries of fictional characters
into the heart of a poet

What if I am a lunar moth
darting in between the laughs in your teeth
your breath damp and moist on my wings

What if you were the scientist
that took all his pain put it on the head of an atom
and exploded that atom into a moon

What if I am that moon
orbiting you like an original stalker

What if you are some unlikely angel
sent to spawn textile art from the sounds in my ears

What if I am a reincarnated priest
here to avenge your father's stolen legacy

What if your straight line Christian ethics
did not cross the straight lines of Muslim morality
there would be no plaid
no geometric spaces to cage our desires

What if I was in the highlands of San Lucas
and you on the scorched earth of Guatemala
both clutching the teachings of Che Guevara

What if you are
Che Guevara or Shaka or Malcolm
or Martin
and I an unholy war of passion

What if I was a petrified starfish
balancing on a too short appendage
that cannot reach you

What if we were knocking knees
under a tabletop of botanas then
swimming like Mayan dolphins through a rainforest canopy

What if we were triple darkness
spinning on the axis of creation
the genesis of friction the split of the nucleus
the divide of the neutron
what if we were there

Before Things Fell Apart before Gorée Island
you a Yoruba yam farmer and
I the daughter of a Hausa market lady

But, but what if I was the red clay
that grew those yams and yellow pineapples
and you were a pineapple worshipper

What then?

Light Spectrum

I

A masculine light spectrum
Ultraviolet man with infrared tongue
Blinking vertical strobes
Rockets shooting into my frontal and posterior lobes
Are you the return of the mother ship?
      the second Christ coming cosmic?
Like astrophysics I'm attracted like magnetic filaments
Like astral- physics I too crave the charge of
a positive cylinder
Like astral physics sometimes I go subatomic effect
chemical change
And then I remember
You are not my lover!

II

20 billion miles from heaven
a breathing light spectrum reflects a dying sun
May I ask: How did my farther become a colorless penguin
      waddling the dessert sky
      looking for his reflection in a falling star?
He found your face riding the wings of Saturn
Are you the return of Jesus,
the Second Christ Coming Cosmic?
At once, I am a child skipping into the light
I stumble when I posthumously remember that
you are not my lover!

III

Two a.m. I become space traveler
 swallowing constellations like a circus act
your inter-galactic girl
a victim of perverse gravity
First I shudder reckless twitches
then rapid frequencies
vibrato lifting me out of this crater I call my body
          to the other side of MC Squared
I am combustion
hydrogen and helium gas
My insides imploding
bubbling peroxide
I get ulcers waiting for you to touch me
Then I fatally remember that
you are not my lover

IV

Three a.m. you become space traveler
a victim of reverse gravity
abandoning down bedding
and this planet!
You are a fleshless balding Super Nova
Light is your language
an untouchable spectrum

V

Four a.m. the tug of sonic vacuums pulls us close
Through time tubes we are drawn
Our faces flat from the force
I am wearing a Victoria Secret space suit
You are hovering the circumference of the Black Hole
We lock atoms and begin to spin down a salty energy funnel
Into me you are absorbed
My skin becomes eyes
asteroid neon eclipses

I Left My Dancing Shoes at Home

I don't want to dance with you
prance ideologies with you
debate foxtrot premises
I don't want to waltz with your hidden Stetson shoes
do rose steps with the back of your ankles

I don't want to disco with the black tam
that sits like cocky arrogance atop your head
cha cha with your 1920 hairs *relevé* in your strained brow

I don't want to lunge umbrella bends to Mingus memories
oozing from the tip of your widow's peak

I don't want to dance Dolphy sax with the
vertebrae in your back

I don't want to soft toe on your wide enamel smile or
cakewalk on your 32nd birthday

I don't want to dance with you A *Capella* in your loneliness
solo ovations on *Solid Ground*
vibrato over Natambu sundaes
duet with dented dimples
exist in a drum fist of absolutes

I don't want to sing to you
serenade the ridges of your palate
scat through salivating truths

I don't want to sorrow song down the inner of your throat
yodel revolving turn tables
You are love with no chaser
fire kisses on the rocks
casual fear in sunken eyes

I want to pull your ear to my chest
so my breasts can whisper how wind creeps
through my window nightly to molest my dreams

I want to free muffled howls of two decades past
hiding in the down of your pillow
latent in the angles of your elbows
abyss bowling on the bottoms of your feet

I want to stew us in Gulf of Gumbo
soup our flesh till it falls tender
like crab meat in oyster shell

But I don't want to Boogaloo or minuet
laugh Mexican hat dance
coo pigeon songs
hum in you rhythms

I don't want to lullaby funky chicken
I don't want to
I don't want
I want
I want   with you

Black Widow Spider: Part 1

Today I swallowed Moon.
He was a burnished meal for my widow spider cravings.
He was culinary heat broiling willing flesh.
He became the pop in my frying colon of hope.
He became the orbit in my sweat lodge of desire.

So the sound of my sound is hot
and my nostrils are torch
They're torch lighters!
My speech is smudge stick of thought.
I am a breathing black widow dragon spider of fire!

Today I drank Sun.
He was spirit lava of unconditional rock.
He was black glass of Mogadishu sand.
He was ignited ether in trapped drum hand.
Dynamic in my stunted hypothalamus
he became the comfort of an electric poultice!

So the sound of my sound is hot
and my nostrils are torch
They're torch lighters!
My speech is smudge stick of thought.
I am the succulent cemetery
black widow spider!

Today I ate the golden rays of Shango.
He was voodoo flame of tall language.
His arms were neon appendages of holding,
an intense simmering of ash and dry memories
      a Yoruba comet walking!

Black Widow Spider: Part 2

She flirts with her prey
then she puts him away

Black Widow Spider Spider Black Widow Spider (BWSSBWS)

She flirts with her prey
then she puts him away
(BWSSBWS)

Arachnids' creed one of survival
She waits for her doting husband's arrival
(BWSSBWS)

She lures him close
offers up a toast
whispers you're
the one I love the most
(BWSSBWS)

Intoxicated by her web
silk strings she has for a bed
the ultimate sacrifice her mate must make
to be with those hairy legs of eight
(BWSSBWS)

She believes in holy union
Her mate she must consume
Lilting lashes controversial practices

she'll eat him come high noon
(**BWSSBWS)**

Injects her serum of unsuspecting fate
She taunts addition of nature's plate
One plus one means you've been had
the way my mother ate your dad
(**BWSSBWS)**

The spell she weaves
You can't perceive how they all
crave that fatal bite

They say if I must die and I must die
surely this will make it alright
(**BWSSBWS)**

Soooo the sound of my sound is hot
and my nostrils are torch
they're torch lighters
My speech is smudge stick of thought
I'm a breathing black widow dragon spider of fire!

Japanese Flower

Thank you for touching me like you
do not know me

for stepping softly through me like I am
a chapel and you
a Black man

Maybe born in the mouth of a
Japanese Flower
I watch you chewing Udon noodles and
wonder about the taste of
Kurosawa films

I can tell that I am starting to care
past chemistry
past the choke and crackle of Yoko Ono songs

My mind divides and lays eggs and divides again

"One day you will ask me which is more important, my life or yours? I will say mine and you will walk away not knowing that you are my life."

Khalil Gibran

Fusion

On Finding Fusion

The writings in this section were inspired by my humanitarian husband and our space/time continuum. He ignited the regenerative light within me at a time when I was but an ember.

 Dr. Brown is a medical doctor, a family physician, who is an expert kindler of flames. He sparked the light of a patient population that swelled to over 2000. He views his patients from a 360-degree perspective. For years, Dr. Brown provided home visits to the elderly and shut-in. He is a medicine man who heals with fire.

When I moved to Genesee County, where my husband's medical practice is located, patients welcomed me with bundles of fresh vegetables from their gardens. They brought hand-crocheted wares, wood-worked gifts, and their Flint city warmth. They offered a kindhearted, "Congratulations, welcome to the family!"

While we were courting, I shared with Dr. Brown my vision of a comprehensive educational structure. It was designed with literacy at the center core, surrounded by outer rings representing additional subjects and support services including health, and music. In this plan the educational and social needs of the whole student would be addressed. In turn, Dr. Brown retrieved from his briefcase his similar concentric plan, only healthcare was the nucleus, with literacy, and other social components, including art, comprising the outer rings to address the total needs of the patient.

If I had not been so focused on assessing and comparing the health-centered versus literacy- centered feasibility of our imagined twenty-first century constructs, I might have recognized with amazement that we both were walking around with almost identical blue prints for healing and education.

Therefore, when the patients said, "Welcome to the family," it was on! Literacy classes, art in the office, music, field trips to the grocery store, cooking classes, weight loss, financially incentivized healthy competitions, health fairs, and collaborative workshops became the norm of the James Brown, MD PLC medical practice with me serving as Community Outreach Director. One Saturday afternoon, when I was facilitating a Type 2 Diabetes support group, several patients reported they heard Dr. Brown confess live on the air, (Cumulus Radio) that Mrs. Brown had saved his life. I responded by telling the eager group that Dr. Brown had saved *my* life. At that point, Mr. Jones, an elderly Black man from Georgia said, "Wait, wait here, somebody lying, less y'all saved each other's lives. Is that whatcha sayn?" "Yes, Mr. Jones," I answered with a smile. He said, "Alrightcha then, naw, that's good, that's real good." Everyone laughed.

And so continued the fusion, like two magnetic planets, James was drawn into Semaj and Semaj into James. Together we bent to fit, to compromise, and to expand.

We were electromagnetically pulled into one another's orbit, until our spheres overlapped, collided, merged, and blended into a solar synthesis, mirroring the reflective light of dynamism — a fusion communion. Our combusting energies form a unique universe of creative circular calisthenics, with Dr. Brown painting acrylics on walls and canvases based on my poetry, and me writing poems inspired by his paintings and music. Our many projects, whether in healthcare, education, the arts, science or business, spin on a double brain axis. Our thoughts rotate, make resolutions, and a Black Love galaxy is formed.

Dr. Brown and I were interviewed by Jason Isaacs, Brooklyn, NY-based, Afro-Caribbean artist and educator, for his documentary, *Black Love Project*, which premiered September 2017, in the Delectricity Festival, Charles H. Wright Museum, Detroit.

Jason Isaacs:

What is Black Love?

Semaj Brown:

Black Love conjures images of a black ocean in space. Out of all of that energy, a tsunami rises up, despite all obstacles. It rises up — despite centuries of oppression, lynchings, despite unimaginable heinous sanctions — it rises up to love....

To love under these conditions of immeasurable cruelty is exceptional. I am not saying that Black Love is better than

Irish Love, or Chinese Love or Polish Love. What I am saying: if you can find it within yourself to love yourself despite being systematically programmed to think yourself despicable for hundreds of years, then this is a miracle. Black Love is therefore a question of identity. It is a question of self-love. So, when Black Love does happen, it is miraculous.

Jason Isaacs is a Brooklyn, NY-based, Afro-Caribbean artist and educator. His practice includes theatre, film, photography, storytelling and performance. He has worked at the Royal Court Theatre and the ITV network in the UK, and as an independent filmmaker. Much of his work addresses themes such as racial justice, reimagining cultural traditions, gentrification and displacement.

Between Poem and Drum

Fingers pressing drum
Glorious drum
Beauteous drum
Sacrificed animal skin stretching to marry your hands
Magnificent hands
Valiant basting hands

The brush of your palms against wild hide
Pounded captured hide
Oracle hide is the caress I envy
Drum longings
Remembering
The leathered soul of Djembe
Rhythmed into the heart-pulsed of throb melody
You play to my core
You play to my core
Desire swells like massaged bread dough
You are the polka-dotted flash dreams of my heart

We the humble Crawlers of Light rolled into
a psychedelic chamber of pantomiming pigeons
Primal we roll
into the altered time plane of magnets
composting days into light years

We the humble Crawlers of Light rolled into and
out of the snake hole of shredded Neanderthal fear

We have rolled

      into an adhesive twine of mint dialogue

      into the tilted angle laugh of passion ride

      into the erasable ink tail of swaggered kisses

      into a lunar wave strut of imaginary phases

We the humble Crawlers of Light rolled

      into the airless balloon of flying salmon

      into the funhouse veneer of reflected cravings

      into the high jacketed calisthenics between poem and
drum

      into the capsized warmth of myopic gazing

      into pink vulva clenched veils beneath teeth

See how we roll

See how we roll surrendered friction

      into a hand holding vapor rub

      into the skin of our secret bone shadows

      into our neglect of wanting to be saved

      into scorpion sting of 3rd degree oath

We the Humble Crawlers of Light roll
sand melting liquid glass
into the flaps of tender apparel
From flesh to fluid
we the Humble Crawlers of Light have rolled
two weeks into two centuries

Swag

Throwing my voice through the wall, I watched my reflection adjust and tug at giant butterfly wings I was trying to adhere to my shoulders. "What are you going as?" Stealth, he entered the threshold, his face straight; Zorro eye mask—black suit with matching black shirt, tie, and shoes. His voice lowered to baritone black, "I am going as, as, the pause was a portal teeming with historical possibilities: Hannibal Barca of Carthage, North Africa, born 247 B.C. greatest military strategist of all time, or Imhotep, architect who built the Step Pyramid and was humanities first surgeon, author, sage and Hippocrates mentor. Or, if ideas were trending toward 20th century genius, Dr. George Washington Carver, world famous agricultural scientist and inventor noted for over 1000 discoveries with that very, important little peanut. "I am going as, as, — The Black Man!" I sneezed a cloud of laughter, internally amused considering my quick mind trip down historical lane, a compilation of Black male greatness was best; I nodded in approval; it presented a strong statement. I told him he looked handsome; he did, but also adorable. How often does a 58 year old Black man get to play dress up, and go to a masquerade as a version of his truest self?

They call it swag now, in my day, we called it cool, that cool, that swag was made, manufactured over centuries of oppression, developed from the heat, the pressure of injustices that our men, Black MEN endure daily; it is a cultural survival response that only God, the Ancestors and the Universe could impart.

That cool, that swag has been appropriated, copied for mass production; it is worth billions, trillions for in it is the answer to the question: How can he, the Black Man be a SUPERMAN, a WAKANDA MAN when every fibrous tentacle of society is designed for his destruction? How does he continue to strive, rise and defy reality?

I look at my husband, James Brown, MD and say a quiet prayer of gratitude as he walks tall as a mountain, back unbent in defense of his manhood, our Love, our family, and the humanity of his people, all people. I witness his encounters with brothers, the power of affirmation exchanged between them, in their knowing handshake, we used to call it giving dap, passing the strength to continue on— climb higher, become more enlightened despite the deadly darts of structural and institutional racism. In those few seconds, of ritualistic embrace, there is a hushed humble acknowledgement of those Black Men who could not, who fell to the death traps, and of those Black Men who stood sacrificing everything; it is All demonstrated in the: pull in, push out, grasp hands, thump back handshake micro ceremony. In it is the power of Imhotep, one who comes in peace! These BROTHERS have always been Wakanda, like the Moors, super engineers, the developers who occupied Spain for 800 years, they build. I was just waiting for the movie!

Dissonance of Memory

Did you forget how it was
before the *Big Bang* of matrimony?
How we were sitting apart from ourselves
like two stubborn suburbs
protesting like angry skunks
wishing some biblical flora
would save us from the surge of Eden

Did you forget how you found me?
I was flatter than a single dimension
my palate was an old wall
from an old house layered
with stories of color

Did you forget I transcended your body
like a shower curtain?
stepped past your invisible iron blockade
to pick fears of gangrene like lint
camouflaged them in my raspberry picking basket
and buried them with the curling
fertilizer of family skeletons

Did you forget
the six little opinions that fell
from our mouths full of cinder?

at the same time
in the same manner

We trance walked
burning wicks for nine hours down the boulevard
over the soiled footprints of "I love you"
until the moon grieved mercy
and bowed to release us
and the sparrows
flew calypso formation to salute us

Did you forget how the tones from
your mahogany-stained music lent the
last bit of image
to a desperate planet?
Dessert and sky I drank with raw flames

Oh my sire, my puppeteer
      my marionette, my appendage
      my soulful isomer reflecting
      a beating aorta in the
      corner of a condemned apartment

From the promise of Victoria Fall's renaming
I am the standing lesser daughter of the wind
I have swallowed your eclipses
In me gestates a simmering

"What's a JB?"

"Mother it's his nickname; it's what everybody calls him." My mother was adamant, "I'm not going to call him any such thing! What's a JB?" Is he not an authentic medical doctor? Did he complete training at an accredited medical school?" "Yes, mom, in Family Medicine he completed a three year residency, and graduated from *Wayne State University School of Medicine*."

Mother was unwavering, "That's an excellent school. Dr. Bachelor graduated from there. You know what it takes for a Black man to get in there and then graduate? And he's running around a JB? I will call him Dr. Brown."

Mother made a sharp jester with her hand and lip that cut the air; it indicated the end. But, I was thinking of a logical retort, something that would break through her stance. Mother was not unreasonable, and was usually willing to listen to opposing views if they were steeped in principle. So I ventured with a good measure of confidence, "Do people not have the freedom, (big important word in our home) to be called by what they choose? Is that not part of being self- determined (another huge, meaningful concept?)

"No!" The response came quickly; she barely breathed before countering. "No, not when Dr. Charles Drew loses his life after developing a blood bank and was then refused adequate medical treatment because he is a Black man."

She was full speed like a locomotive with a clear destination, "Not when Dr. Vivian Thomas was denied the right to practice medicine yet he developed all those heart the surgical procedures in the 40s to cure blue blood babies, and he was not recognized until the 70s when he was almost dead! Not after all those sustained incidents of in justice Dr. Charles Wright documented in the book, *The National Medical Association DEMANDS EQUAL OPPORTUNITY Nothing More, Nothing Less!*

No, he does not earn the right to deny his legacy, a legacy paid for in blood. He does not have the right to deny young Black boys and girls the opportunity to hear and see him being called doctor so they will know they too can become doctors. We have to counter the negative images of Black men in every way in every moment. Like I said, I will be calling him Dr. Brown to honor Dr. Charles Drew."

Mother James was born in 1918, a time when Black men were not recognized as men by white society, and becoming a doctor was an accomplishment, a celebration for the entire community. With finality she spoke, "It is disrespectful to be glib about our sacrifices."

Drum Doctor

Introducing…………Drum Doctor!!!
Houdini act of white-light proportions
Icicled illusionist disguised in winterized nice guy costume
Lattice stricken by post 1970's freeze dried Civil Rights age
 Inclement adolescence

Hey… Clandestine vegetable lover!
Acrylic vision painter escape artist
Subterranean rhythm scientist
Inventor of Arborlune™
tree and string instruments serenading
While wearing insulated North Pole wardrobe
While wearing neon dashiki
Under stealth laboratory armor
Under Power House t-shirt
Under skin like disappearing veins of Bermuda Triangle
An underground proud refrigerator

They vowed to – KILL you – Veto You
Those institutional mud pie slashers
Destroyers of masculine courage
Ordered you ink- blotted like Tuskegee Experiment
No wonder your scalpel directs with suspicious passion

But you were quark fast-flurry
Regenerating in a Maccabee hailstorm
Exhaling
the frigid exhaust of Detroit

Chanting Arctic beats from lower Eastside
Suturing yourself after Medical Seminary

Anointed survivor
2nd year Resident iceberg
Skiing past ricocheting bullets at bus stops
with voltage of Middle Passage redemption
Crawling combustion through blizzards
Physician at sub-zero degrees
Endowed with Cryogenics of spiritual dimensions
Concealed in emotional permafrost
Hidden by shards of frozen mirrors
Buried in sleet from heaven
Liquid Nitrogen smoke visibility
with a North Star allegiance

You became The Cold that Warms
Drum Doctor!!! Drum Doctor!!!
Houdini act of white-light proportions
of push button avalanches
Preserved in Urban Boreal

May I candlelight your fossilized dreams?
Drum Doctor!!! Drum Doctor!!!
Your prayer is a subcutaneous lava moan
To breathe swirling cadences through
frosted tubes of broken stethoscopes

Your vision is a super natural velvet sleep
You yearn to wade in the tepid vineyard of magenta sky

Ceremonial Ankh wearer
Testimony from a welded physician
from the sprouted tundra of Bewick and Mack
Moon-bone connected to a glaciered heart
Connected to a managed fear in practitioner's silk
You hold the bottomless tree bearing pulse
You wear the generosity of capped mountains

Marked by biochemistry of burning genius
Genius burning biochemistry
You melted yourself down
Melted yourself down
and fashioned a geyser
into the fire black healing potion
From which I sip

Republished from *Poet in the House: The Poet in Residence Program: A Decade of Collaboration between Broadside Poets and the Detroit Public Library* Copyright 2005 Broadside Press, Detroit

Remember Re mem ber ing

Before the beginning
before the rising sun
before the thought of future
before the prayer of separation
world torn from worlds
before sea crept from earth by moon beam
before moon
before dessert
when all was a black dot.

Before the beginning
when motion was the only religion
lonely then too
I evoked a cover folded you into a womb and
beckoned beckoned
for you to form me from under an ignited sky of ocean.
And in the rich exchange of cyclic respiration
and in the deep marbling of spirit
we created the air and
spilled our progeny into the soundless flight of flickering
novae.

Before the beginning
before I became aware of myself you were there
my beloved my projection my constant.
You were the light floating a walk across a montage of
darkness.

Before my brain could see

you were the humble mind of space
my betrothed.

You are the fourth dimension
time in a feminine envelope the clock of my spirit

my germ dormant is the tick of your memory
theology of heart.

For 66 trillion eons I searched the unseen for you
exiled from my center. Oh my core,
Do you not recognize your living ancestor?
I am the broth of your tears.
You look to me through the glazed fever of forget
Alzheimer's of the soul!
Even when you were sightless you were yet a bed of vision.
Spiritual amnesia is surely my sorrow.

Explore the X-ray Light of Not Seeing

I see differently from most. I am not referring to my opinions or my outlook on life. I am suggesting that the actual visual images my brain conjures and brings into focus are decidedly different. If what I am seeing appears outlandish, or preposterous, Fun House-like or Alice in Wonderlandish, then it is most likely a brain mirage that no one else sees. I have learned to camouflage and compensate. My antidote to seeing things differently is to remain silent about the obtuse images I am seeing and simply carry on. Ignore and proceed, ignore and proceed. Ignore and proceed has a rhythm that has allowed me to navigate with less social upheaval and explanation.

Not only am I seeing differently. My memory betrays me daily. Some things just do not stick. It has been this way since I was a child. I learned to swim at eight years old, received a Red Cross intermediate card and returned to the deep end the next summer to almost drown. This oddness repeated with bike riding. Now, I am proficient in both activities, but it is one of those things that make you go hmmm.

In Brooklyn, I was asked to view video footage shot by friend, international artist, Jasmine Murrell. I tell Jasmine it is simply beautiful: I have always loved autumn leaves, the oranges, the yellows, those rust tones. It's my favorite time of year. Jasmine pauses and says, "Really Semaj?" Her wide smile breaks into a laugh. She goes on marveling about how my mind works.

I am sitting quietly wondering about the source of her amazed enthusiasm. Well, it turns out the video was of decaying industrial buildings and there were no leaves, no trees. Go figure!

Then there was the time I was introduced to a lovely lady five times in one month. I know this because she told me (show off) on the sixth time. I was standing beside her at an art gallery, and I turned toward her to offer my hand and introduce myself. She said, "I know you, Semaj. We worked on the such and such committee and we were at the so and so together." Embarrassed, I offered my warmest smile and said, "Of course, how have you been since last week?"

Since I now know I fall somewhere on the *face blindness* spectrum, described by Dr. Olive Sachs, physician, professor of neurology, and best-selling author, I simply pretend to recognize everyone I encounter! "How are you?" I exclaim with animated anticipation. Unintended consequences are the puzzled looks on some folk's faces while they struggle to place how they know me when they really do not. What is a partially face blind poet to do? Social media has been a helpful tool, as it pairs photos with names. One of my very dear Facebook friends has a cat for a profile picture. I wonder when I see her again, will my mind configure the image of a striped, puffy ball of fur.

Recently, some version of my mind's shape-shifting resulted in comedy. My then new friend, Dr. Sharon Simeon, who is an artist and professor, presented me with a gift, accompanied with the tender words: "This pin," she explained, pausing slightly, "represents freedom. I was inspired to give this to you because your work, your poetry, symbolizes the freedom you give to me, my daughters — and all of us." I was moved, as the gift was so unexpected.

Carefully, I unfold the tissue to find a lovely piece of jewelry. I stare at it for a few moments, overwhelmed by Dr. Sharon's intention, then exclaim, "Oh, Sharon, this is lovely! A flying unicorn swimming under water! It is beautiful!" I am holding the pin between finger and thumb, mesmerized as it seems to be unveiling, morphing, or I am beginning to see it more clearly. "Silly me," I add. "It's not a flying unicorn swimming under water. It is a multi- dimensional lizard – no, a squirrel that has scales." I point to the scales and ask, "However did you find a pin that challenges conventional assumptions?"

Sharon attempts a logical reply. She utters softly, like thinking out loud, but to herself, "Well birds and reptiles are on the same evolutionary trajectory." Her hands are gesturing the possibilities, her head giving a reasonable tilt of consideration. "This is an amazing piece, Sharon; it is some type of super squirrel. This art is spatially magical, definable, but fluid!" Abruptly, Sharon stops her internal/external meanderings, and breaks from this alternate universe of suggestions. Sharon, the professor emerges, and with quickened speed, removes the pen from my grasp, flips it around, from front to back, then up to down. The flick of her hand and expression on her face said, "Look!"

Oh, my goodness, I had been looking at the pin upside down and wrong side out. There the lacey pewter jewelry was in front of me, suspended in space, held steady by Sharon's firm grip. It was at an optimal distance so that I could see clearly that this lovely piece of metal art was a bird, a beautiful bird. "It's a bird!" I said, as if it were the rarest of all things, surprise lingering in the air. We fell into uncontrollable laughter. Giggles erupted into almost screams of hilarity. Bent, we were trying to catch our breath, stifling shrieks.

Seeing differently allowed me to see him. I saw him! I did not see a Millennium Drummer making beats on the Detroit River, waves jumping off the concrete of Hart Plaza. I saw him. I did not see a burgeoning poet, reading awkward images at Black World Books on East Jefferson Ave. across from Belle Isle. I saw him; but I did not see the stethoscope hanging and white doctor's coat flinging, as he advocated for his patients against institutional injustice — though he was all that and more. I did not see JB. I did not see JB, the name he was called, and called himself in all the city's poetry venues: the coffee house days of Café Mahogany in Harmony Park, Bert's on Sunday nights in the Eastern Market, Broadside Press Poetry Theater Workshops with Willie Williams as maître d' of poems, first Sunday Poetry Roundtable; Ron Allen cooking dinners of baked chicken and roasted vegetables with sautéed verse at UU Church, round table with Sonya and Wardell and Darolyn and Kaleemah. I saw him, but I did not see a man. I did not see a man. I saw a mountain.

A real mountain, I swear. I saw a mountain, complete with earth and trees growing from his bald head.

His legs were chunky roots. Of course, I told no one, no one! Many years of training served me well: ignore and proceed, ignore and proceed, and carry on, carry on, carry on! After we were married, Dr. Brown painted a beautiful acrylic entitled, *Eye Storm*. I gazed into the center of the center, and was activated. I penned, "The Mountain and the Steaming Monsoon."

The Mountain and the Steaming Monsoon

Once upon a time, seven long years into the future, there was an honorable mountain who was also a man. Quite abruptly, the man-mountain felt an unusual burst of heat. The mountain's icy apex had begun to melt, releasing fresh water streams from two wide-set fissures. Tributaries meandered down the rocky terrain, giving the distinct impression the mountain was in a perpetual state of river cry. He, the mountain, prided himself as a rugged naturalist, and thus became increasingly concerned about his image. The noble mountain was being worn down by environmental problems associated with erosion. This was indeed true, for he had his bald head to prove it. The industrious mountain enlisted the assistance of his cousin, Plate Tectonics, who assisted in breaking the mountain off from the Western Range, to journey in search of that much rumored, controversial global warming heat source.

Burdened, he traveled into the millennium with a sure-footed goat attached to his back. His cliffs donned prickly pine bushes that passed for unkempt facial hair. A tree that doubled as a unicorn's scepter and weather vane extended from the middle of his brow. Dangling, uprooted roots hung from his ears and from between his toes.

Suddenly, the mountain's tears of streaming rivers flooded into fast rising rapids. Unknowingly, the rocky mass of elevation was approaching the Seventh Dimensional Shift! He had crossed over into an alternate reality, the Forbidden Zone of Semaj. Semaj, the steamy monsoon maker was a cauldron of terrestrial storms and fiery combustions. She was a feminine creature with twin tempests exploding behind her placid gaze.

The mountain-who-was-a-man spied, captivated from the inflatable raft deep inside his cave. He was mesmerized by the monsoon's dark flaming hair and whirl pooling sparks of gale force winds. Never before had he seen an ocean spring from a being, ignite into fire, then extinguish into smoky vapors drawn straw-like through invisible portals back into its sublime origin. Wow! In a strange poetic wondrous way, he felt that he knew her and so he intoned, "Sistah, sistah, don't I know you, sistah?"

She responded by burning, blowing him hot coals of beaded rain. Unbeknownst to the steaming monsoon, the mountain-who-was-a-man was also the wisest dust gatherer of the last one thousand years, as well as an expert juggler and Family Physician, who knew like no other how to handle the ancient elements of fire and water.

First, he concocted a formula of golden mountain dust to secure and temper her magnetic scalding to a warm glow.

Second, the mountain made rich fertile mud from her scarlet torrents to harvest a garden of hope, of figs, of diamonds.

Finally, the mountain took one courageous step beyond the sweltering veils into the nucleus of the monsoon's eye to discover and marvel at a beautiful woman, vulnerable beneath her garments of seaweed and ash. It was a goodly union. They married, and my sources tell me they reside in some exotic place called Flint, Michigan, where they are perfectly domesticated, joyful.

———————————

This story, "The Mountain and the Steaming Monsoon," was inspired by looking into Eye Storm, an acrylic painting rendered by Dr. James Brown (2003).

Freedom Tree Song

This tree is free
This tree is free
From hanging tombs
And nooses as costumes

It walks and talks as witness!
A time that time can't forget this!
This tree is love is life
Its skin the bark of strife

Extends it hands as leaves
To untangle knots we grieve

This tree is friend
as air it does command
So we may breathe breathe breathe

Chorus:
Breathe beyond the blows of history
Breathe into the wind of destiny

Breathe the fire from our eyes
Breathe breath into the child that dies

Breathe breathe breathe

This tree is free
This tree is free

We grow perennial souls
We grow clouds for rain
We are sun drying pain
This tree is free
This tree is me

My arms as branches
My heart expansive in the hearth of this Earth
This tree is free
This tree is
Making music harmony
From we, from we free

_____

The poem, "Freedom Tree Song" *was inspired after listening to and marveling at the invention, The Arborlune™, a percussion/string musical instrument made from found tree branches in our backyard constructed by Dr. James Brown.*

Epilogue

Social Justice Eats the Entire Pi (π):
Arguing for Integrated /Interdisciplinary Pedagogy

Amphibians understand social justice principles. Their understanding is exhibited by restraint. Consider this Native American wisdom: A frog does not drink up the pond in which it lives.

In addition, the frog will not pour toxic waste into the pond. The frog will not manufacture addictive sugar drinks, aggressively advertise them as alternatives to water, feed those drinks to guppies, and then watch their guppy babies swell into preventable diseases. A frog will not deny the scourge of climate change as it is being cooked alive by carbon dioxide emissions. That frog will not attend university, study glacial water science, and never once examine the impact of polar thaw on the disenfranchised Inuit people. But then, what does a frog know? Perhaps the frog knows not to make indiscriminate distinctions between science and art, and perhaps it knows not to create constructs of academic hierarchy that result in the truncated pedagogy of competition and disconnection, rather than cooperation and interconnection. To date, it is still a matter of debate exactly what frogs know, but all agree: a frog knows not to drink up the pond in which it lives.

The Earth as community is a dynamic organism, a free, living thing. Her constituents, elements, and social groupings suspend like an evolving cell in a naturally occurring universe. Earth's spontaneity evokes scholarship. It is a mystery to be investigated by science, explored and expanded by art. The science to which I refer is not hard or soft, nor is it natural or social, but science without the peril of partition. The segmenting off of physical science, life science, justice science, and the arts or art science engenders schisms that foster a calcified conceptualization of natural phenomena.

Fragmented theories and non-reflective policies give rise to the decline of diverse populations. Hence, the extinct Titicaca water frog, the shattered communities of urban blight, and the anonymity of rural deprivation. Tentacles of discontinuity are systemic, extending from university, to legislature, to corporate structures, to the justice system, and on. Social science provides the moral compass, the critical balance to technological and scientific advances. Separating social science, and by extension social justice, from the so-called natural sciences of chemistry, earth science, astronomy, life science, and physics, promotes innovation without concern for consequence. Even the arena of business would be enhanced by the inclusion of the sciences and arts. Such an amalgam would foster a panoramic corporate consciousness that is sustainable and profitable, without the stain of exploitation.

To be human is to be of nature — a point of view which is not reflected in the classification model of our current educational systems. I assert the study of social justice is a natural science, and should not be relegated to confines of social science. Likewise, so-called natural sciences are indeed social. After all, humans are as naturally occurring as a frog, or any ionized atom studied in chemistry. This is undeniable.

The human body is a magnum conductor of electricity, and humans are as naturally occurring as a molecule of H_2O. We mortals, like the Earth's surface, are comprised of 75% water, and are thus walking, talking rivers. Humans even organize themselves into super "charged" clusters called families. Similarly, electromagnetic fields gather "socially," directly impacting our natural existence.

Moreover, social justice is as rigorous and complex a discipline as quantifiable physics. In fact, we *are the definition* of physics: the study of matter moving through space across time exposed to heat and energy. This is the description of the *migration of peoples* across drought lands, where the matter in question is humans, and temperatures extreme.

Time, technology, and the challenges of this millennium necessitate the removal of blinders. Silo thinkers and the linear policies they breed are obsolete. It is the charge of sentient beings to usher in fusion paradigms. The call for fundamental structural changes in the current knowledge industry is paramount.

Imagine learning through the diameter of a circle of awareness where piercing across the circle, the diameter is the intersection of multiple genres, a sort of Pi = 3.14 representation of academic studies, where Pi is the ratio of the circumference of a circle, (the circle as selected subject matter) to its diameter (seemingly disparate genres).

Ultimately, we students of the universe vie for something beyond interconnectedness — the recognition that in every subject matter there is extant all subject matter. This is the reality — as in the quark of the macrocosm, there exists the identical quark of the microcosm. The sameness in particulate supports a fundamental paradox: homogeneity traverses the natural sphere of diversity.

In the kernel of this understanding, there is a dissolution formula, a process that unhinges the vile precepts of xenophobia, and its violent parade of isms. To grow a planet of techies surrounded by a subset-island of artsy-types, with social scientists orbiting the stratosphere, and commercialization rivaling gravitational force, is much like trying to grow a garden where the soil is to the left, the seeds are to the right, the sun in a box, water somewhere over the rainbow, only to then, collectively and inharmoniously grieve the absence of a verdant harvest.

In the innovative imagined space of Social Justice, clarification is crystalized. Apprentices of the universe understand gerrymandering of academic canons. We realize margins are but constructs, similar to other margin-making inventions — the making of race and designer poverty, the abhorrent dissection of a people to form a Tutsi, a Hutus, the invention and mass distribution of plastics, the turning of water into a commodity, a poison, a war.

If ever there is a resolution toward the whole, a coalescence of that which has been ripped apart, a reverse combustion, it will happen in the realm of social justice.
Social Justice is magnetic ground where estranged disciplines can reunify, and speak the common language of natural phenomena. As an open harbor, the gravitational need to resolve to the whole, to return to origins, and break down contrived borders is unstoppable. All stretched rubber bands eventually collapse into themselves, or they break. When art recognizes itself as science, and has conversation, miraculous things happen. When math speaks literature, transformations conspire. Walls fall when dance knows it is a moving constellation of cosmos connective tissue doing the Boogie Woogie of economic, global commerce. Art is magnifying glass, and microscope; it is biofeedback; it renders the hard data. Artists are scientific messengers — the griots, the raconteurs, the jesters, the observers of the day.

Quantum wave theory and social justice both rise in the ocean of imagination. They are a carved poetry, a centrifuge, a persistent extractor and editor of false assumptions and unsupported hypotheses. Together, they conjoin the spectrum of human potential, and rush into the fertile gulf of possibility. There is an ebb and flow between inspiration and calculation.

When social justice is art, the community learns the quantum mechanics of glass blowing destiny, transforming the dilapidated sands from urban and Appalachian decay into re-imagined vessels of measureable light. Like a tenacious muse, social justice movements instigate toward freedom, drawing a path similar to phototropic plants that follow the arc of the sun from east to west. Social justice is a global march of imagination, straight from the artist's laboratory.

The power to re-imagine one's condition is innate, as primal as species reproduction or the quest for liberty. Communal capacity dreams, and then paints those dreams into a new cultural formation, onto a self-determined canvas. This is masterful experimentation. The yield?
Music of homeostasis, choir of croaking frogs, and the harmony of access in healthy, sustainable societies.

About the Author

Semaj Brown graduated from Cass Technical High School, a college preparatory magnet school in Detroit, where for four years; students are submerged in a specific concentration of study. Semaj selected the curriculum of avocational music, which was a discipline that included ensemble music classes such as symphony orchestra, math and the sciences. After attending Grambling State University in Louisiana, Semaj earned a Bachelor of Arts degree in Biological Sciences from Wayne State University in 1986. During post bachelor and graduate studies years, Semaj completed literature, writing, and education classes.

As a young educator in the Detroit Public Schools, Semaj focused on designing innovative science curricula. She served as a curriculum developer for the Creative and Gifted Department, and developed the Area A Initiative, *Teaching from a Dialectical Perspective,* collaborating with fellow chemistry teacher Valerie Boniswa Brock. Semaj created several other programs, including, *Rodentia Studies and Protocols,* which involved a partnership with Wayne State University's Department of Veterinary Studies, and *Investigations into Drosophila: Genetics Probe for 6th Graders,* funded by COMPACT, as well as the exhibit, *The Cell as a City.* Semaj also was involved in the River Rough Water Testing Restoration Project, and was selected to be part of a State committee to establish a data base in Biology education for the Skillman Foundation.

Semaj's students won multiple local and international science fair awards, including first place in the NOBCCHE Science

Bowl in Chicago. As a science educational consultant, Semaj applied her integrated pedagogy, and was instrumental in assisting Timbuktu Academy of Science and Technology

to achieve the Golden Apple Award, elevating science standardized test scores from statistically negligible.

Semaj's teaching methods, which she coined as *Web Theory,* merge art and science, left-and right brain modalities, to challenge conventions in science, health education, the literary arts, and theater.

As a girl, Semaj enjoyed a wide range of cultural experiences, playing violin in the Highland Park Chamber Orchestra, and spending summers in Stratford, Ontario, studying Shakespeare. Her mother, the late Mrs. Bessie L. James, a classical pianist and Pan-Africanist, nurtured Semaj's appreciation for world cultures. Home science laboratory explorations expanded Semaj's imagination, so that by college, she was identifying patterns in disparate disciplines — math, science, literature, art, and music – seeking a more integrated approach to knowledge. She was becoming a paradigm shifter, a creative innovator.

As artist, Semaj belongs to the group of Broadside Lotus Press poets referred to as *progeny* or next generation, who emerged after the Broadside Press Legacy poets of the 1960s and 70s, Dudley Randall, Sonia Sanchez, Haki Madhubuti, Audre Lorde, Etheredge Knight, and Pulitzer Prize recipient Gwendolyn Brooks. Semaj has served twice as a Broadside Press poet-in-residence, at the Detroit Public Library and at the Arts League of Michigan. Semaj developed the programming, *Extreme Poetry,* which addressed persons in drug rehabilitation programs in Detroit. She was also invited by the Life Skills Social Services Division of Contra Costa County, California to bring her arts/science poetry workshop, *Everything Is Word,* to youth who were transitioning out of the foster care system.

Throughout the 80s and 90s, Semaj performed her poetry nationally, often with live bands, at universities, invited by Women Studies, Africana Studies, English Literature professors, and Diversity Departments, as well as at libraries, museums and other venues. In 2002, her Tongue, Tongued CD ushered in the Tongue, Tongued concert with The Last Poets as her guests at the Millennium Theater in Southfield, Michigan. Semaj's poetry was featured in the poetry play, "Womb Tongue" (2003), directed by Sandra Hines, choreographed by Kimberli Boyd, music by Jon Muhammad, Sponsored by the Arts League of Michigan and National Endowment for the Arts. In 2004, Semaj was invited to read her poetry at the Women's International Word Dub Conference in Toronto, Canada. She has recorded and collaborated with noted composers, musicians and artists such as the late, great Faruq Z. Bey, and late visionary playwright Ron Allen, Ras Kente, Sunkaru Clifford Sykes, Issa Abralameem, Wayne Wardlow, Ella Singer, Riva Stewart, Fonz, Michelle Jahra McKinney, the late Robyn Sampson and Laurie Ford, Dawud, the Last Poets, and international fine artist, Jasmine Murrell. Semaj's poem, "Wave Rock," was made into an art video by Jasmine Murrrell. The soundtrack, an anthem for oppressed people, has become a Brooklyn favorite.

Since her marriage to James Brown MD, Board Certified Family Physician, Semaj has collaborated in many long-term projects to urge their Flint community towards healthier lifestyles. She became the Community Outreach Director for James Brown, MD PLC. (2004-2007), authoring the employee manual, and writing copy for radio programs on *Cumulus WCK 1570 SuperTalk*. Her numerous voiceovers brought levity to the broadcasts. She introduced a popular segment to listeners: *What's for Dinner, Mrs. Brown?* Semaj and her husband cofounded the Planted Kingdom™ Project and Health Collectors™ LLC to promote wellness in the community through science/art applications. Semaj organized three major health conferences sponsored by Dr. Brown's medical practice.

Semaj has used poetry as a health education tool to help her husband save his patients' lives. As ambassador to the *American Heart Association,* she designed and implemented 70 workshops for the community. These programs were held at Dr. Brown's medical practice, in churches, community centers, the YWCA, schools, and throughout Genesee County. In 2012, Semaj wrote the poetic curriculum, *Butterfly Building: A Self-Actualization Program for Women.* She is also the author of *Feasts and Fables of the Planted Kingdom: A Vegetarian Gluten Free Story Cookbook and Lyrical CD*, which is the foundational material for her play, "Onion Revolt," a one-woman comedy in which vegetables come alive as rock-stars and activists. Dr. Brown created the original music for the play. "Onion Revolt" debuted in 2014, hosted by the Flint Youth Theater.

In 2016, heeding the call of the Detroit Independent Freedom Schools Movement (DIFS) at the Charles H. Wright Museum of African American History, Semaj constructed a pop-up science laboratory, with a curriculum entitled *Seven Biology/Chemistry Experiments.* Dr. Brown served as medical career consultant to the eager students. They transformed the mundane classroom into an exciting space of science exploration.

Also in 2016, Semaj was the creative director of an arts program funded by the Pierian Foundation, *Project Water Us,* implemented at the Boys and Girls Club (BGC) of Greater Flint.

Semaj collaborated with Flint Chapter Pierians, Edith Withey, Diane Kirksey, and Velynda Makhene to implement workshops that revealed how protest art, or art of resistance, impacted struggles for freedom and self-determination during the eras of Enslavement, the Harlem Renaissance, Civil Rights and the emergence of Hip Hop. Semaj is the chapter president of the Flint Pierians, Inc.

In 2018, Semaj returned to the *BGC as educational consultant and educator* with an art/science program, *Creating a Vegetable Consciousness™ through Science, Craft Work, Visual Arts, Music, and Theater.* This was a Planted Kingdom™ Project of Health Collectors™ LLC, and was sponsored by the generosity of Susan A. Kornfield.

Recently Semaj created "Mother Ocean," an epic poem, which was inspired by an exhibit of photographs by Jerry Taliaferro, featured at the Flint Institute of Arts (FIA) in 2017. She presented the poem at the FIA Tenth Anniversary

Gala, marking her return to public poetry performances. Later, Semaj would perform a second iteration of the poem in her original production," By Ocean By Fire: An Odyssey in African American History and Culture," at the Charles H. Wright Museum of African American History, to benefit DIFS and the Charles H. Wright Museum. Dr. Brown served as musical director at both presentations.

In January 2019, as a member of Zeta Phi Beta Sorority, Incorporated, Zeta Beta Zeta, Semaj delivered the keynote address at the 99th annual Founders' Day Celebration of the Michigan State Organization, Angela Philmore, state director. Also in 2019, Semaj was asked to create a poem to honor Flint Mayor, Dr. Karen Weaver, on her birthday. The poem, entitled "Fire Weaver," was an allegorical fable that drew connections between ancient African iron forgers and Flint steel factory workers. It concludes with images of Mayor Dr. Weaver garnering the power of fire to help resolve the Flint water crisis.

This year, Semaj will celebrate the release of this book in a performance on May 18th, at the Charles H. Wright Museum of African American History in Detroit. Dr. Brown will join her as musical director of the production, featuring his original musical invention, the Arborlune[TM].